Credit Risk Measurement

Wiley Frontiers in Finance

Series Editor: Edward I. Altman, New York University

Credit Risk
Measurement

New Approaches to Value at Risk and Other Paradigms

Anthony Saunders

John Wiley & Sons, Inc.
New York • Chichester • Weinheim • Brisbane • Singapore • Toronto

Published by John Wiley & Sons, Inc.
Published simultaneously in Canada.

This publication is designed to provide accurate and authoritative
information in regard to the subject matter covered. It is sold with the
understanding that the publisher is not engaged in rendering professional
services. If professional advice or other expert assistance is required, the
services of a competent professional person should be sought.

Library of Congress Cataloging-in-Publication Data:

Saunders, Anthony.
    Credit risk measurement : new approaches to value at risk and
other paradigms / Anthony Saunders.
       p. cm. — (Wiley frontiers in finance)
    Includes bibliographical references and index.
    ISBN 0-471-35084-2 (cloth)
    1. Bank loans. 2. Bank management. 3. Credit—Management.
  4. Risk management. I. Title. II. Series.
HG1641.S33   1999
332.1'2'0684—dc21   99-11514

Printed in the United States of America.

10 9 8 7 6 5 4 3 2 1

Preface

In recent years, enormous strides have been made in the art and science of credit risk measurement and management. Much of the energy in this area has resulted from dissatisfaction with traditional approaches to credit risk measurement and with the current Bank for International Settlements (BIS) regulatory model. Specifically, under the current regulatory structure, established by the BIS in 1988 in cooperation with the world's major central banks, and implemented in January 1993, virtually all private-sector loans are subject to an 8 percent capital requirement with no account being taken of either: (1) credit quality differences among private-sector borrowers or (2) the potential for credit risk reduction via loan portfolio diversification.

The new models—some publicly available and some partially proprietary—seek to offer alternative "internal model" approaches to measuring the credit risk of a loan or a portfolio of loans. As with market risk in 1993, a debate currently rages as to the extent to which internal models can replace regulatory models—and in which areas of credit risk measurement and management.

Much of the research in this area has been quite technical and not easily accessible to the interested practitioner, student, economist, or regulator. The aim of this book is to bring the debate regarding the "value" of the new internal credit risk models to a wider audience. In doing so, I have tried to simplify the technical details and analytics surrounding these models, while concentrating on their underlying economics and economic intuition.

In many cases, providing a full description of the new models has been hampered because of their semiproprietary nature and because only parts of the modeling approach have been made publicly available through working papers, published papers, and other outlets. Thus, many model details are "translucent" rather than transparent.[1] I have tried to be as accurate as possible in describing the different models. Where the full details of a modeling approach are uncertain or unclear, I have used the description "type," as in a "KMV-type" model. This is an indication (1) of my understanding of the general approach used or (2) that a similar approach has been followed in the publicly available literature by other researchers.

This literature is very new. At the time of writing, it can be regarded as being at a stage similar to that of market risk modeling when J.P. Morgan's RiskMetrics first appeared in 1994.

The book follows a "building blocks" approach. Chapter 1 provides the motivation for the recent growth of the new credit risk models. Chapter 2 briefly overviews traditional models of credit risk measurement. Chapters 3 through 8 examine the approaches of the new models to evaluating individual borrower (or counterparty) credit risk and to the valuation of individual loans. One of the major features of the newer models is that they consider credit risk in a portfolio context; consequently, Chapters 9 through 12 examine the application of modern portfolio theory concepts to evaluation of the risk of loan portfolios. Finally, many of the new models are equally applicable to assessing credit risk off-balance-sheet as well as on-balance-sheet. Thus, Chapters 13 and 14 look at the application of the new models to assessing the risk of derivative contracts, and the use of such contracts in managing credit risk.

I thank a number of people for their encouragement, insights, and comments. They include, in no particular order: Mark Carey, Lazarus Angbazo, Frank Diebold, Larry Wall, Jim Gilkeson, Kobi

---

[1] I'd like to thank Stuart Turnbull of CIBC for this description.

Boudoukh, Anthony Morris, Sinan Cebonoyan, Marti Subrah-manyam, Ranga Sundaram, Anil Bangia, Anand Srinivasan, Sreedhar Bharath, Alex Shapiro, and Til Schuermann. Finally, I'd like to thank my colleague, Ed Altman, for encouraging me to look into this area and for keeping the "torchlight" of credit risk analysis burning during the past 30 years. Nevertheless, at the end of the day, I take full responsibility for any errors of omission or commission that may be found here.

ANTHONY SAUNDERS

New York, New York
May 1999

Contents

List of Abbreviations

AE	average exposure
BIS	Bank for International Settlements
BSM	Black–Scholes–Merton Model
CAPM	capital asset pricing model
CIBC	Canadian Imperial Bank of Commerce
CLNs	credit-linked notes
CLOs	collateralized lending obligations
CMR	cumulative mortality rate
CSFP	Crédit Suisse Financial Products
CYC	current yield curve
DM	Default Mode or Model
EC	European Community
EDF	expected default frequency
EVA	economic value added
FIs	financial institutions
FV	future value
FX	foreign exchange
IDR	implied debenture rating
LAS	Loan Analysis System (KPMG)
LGD	loss given default

LIBOR	London Interbank Offered Rate
MD	modified duration
MMR	marginal mortality rate
MPT	modern portfolio theory
MRC	marginal risk contribution
MTM	Mark-to-Market Model
NASD	National Association of Securities Dealers
NPV	net present value
OAEM	other assets especially mentioned
OBS	off-balance-sheet
OCC	Office of the Comptroller of the Currency
OECD	Organization for Economic Cooperation and Development
OPM	option-pricing model
OTC	over-the-counter
RAROC	risk-adjusted return on capital
RBC	risk-based capital
Repo	repurchase agreement
RHS	right-hand side
RN	risk-neutral
ROA	return on assets
ROE	return on equity
RORAC	return on risk-adjusted capital
SBC	Swiss Bank Corporation
SPV	special-purpose vehicle
VAR	value at risk
WACC	weighted-average cost of capital
WARR	weighted-average risk ratio
ZYC	zero yield curve

Credit Risk
Measurement

Chapter **1**

Why New Approaches to Credit Risk Measurement and Management?

INTRODUCTION

In recent years, a revolution has been brewing in the way credit risk is both measured and managed. Contradicting the relatively dull and routine history of credit risk, new technologies and ideas have emerged among a new generation of financial engineering professionals who are applying their model-building skills and analysis to this area.

The question arises: Why now? There are at least seven reasons for this sudden surge in interest.

STRUCTURAL INCREASE IN BANKRUPTCIES

Although the most recent recession hit at different times in different countries, most bankruptcy statistics showed a significant increase in bankruptcies, compared to the prior recession. To the extent that there has been a permanent or structural increase in bankruptcies worldwide—possibly due to the increase in global competition—accurate credit risk analysis becomes even more important today than in the past.

DISINTERMEDIATION

As capital markets have expanded and become accessible to small and middle market firms (e.g., it is estimated that as many as

1

20,000 U.S. companies have actual or potential access to the U.S. commercial paper market), the firms or borrowers "left behind" to raise funds from banks and other traditional financial institutions (henceforth, FIs) are increasingly likely to be smaller and have weaker credit ratings. Capital market growth has produced a "winner's curse" effect on the credit portfolios of traditional FIs.

MORE COMPETITIVE MARGINS

Almost paradoxically, despite a decline in the average quality of loans (due to the second reason above), interest margins or spreads, especially in wholesale loan markets, have become very thin—that is, the risk–return trade-off from lending has gotten worse. A number of reasons can be cited, but an important factor has been the enhanced competition for lower-quality borrowers, such as from finance companies, much of whose lending activity has been concentrated at the higher risk–lower quality end of the market.

DECLINING AND VOLATILE VALUES OF COLLATERAL

Concurrent with the recent Asian crisis, banking crises in well-developed countries such as Switzerland and Japan have shown that property values and real asset values are very hard to predict and to realize through liquidation. The weaker and more uncertain collateral values are, the more risky lending is likely to be. Indeed, current concerns about "deflation" worldwide have accentuated concerns about the value of real assets such as property and other physical assets.

THE GROWTH OF OFF-BALANCE-SHEET DERIVATIVES

The growth of credit exposure, or counterparty risk, because of the phenomenal expansion of derivative markets, has extended the need for credit analysis beyond the loan book. In many of the very largest U.S. banks, the notional (not market) value of their off-balance-sheet exposure to instruments such as over-the-counter (OTC) swaps and forwards is more than ten times the size of their loan books. Indeed, the growth in credit risk off the balance sheet was one of the main reasons for the introduction, by the Bank for International Settlements (BIS), of risk-based capital (RBC) requirements in 1993. Under the BIS system, banks have to hold a capital requirement based on the marked-to-market current value of each OTC derivatives contract (so-called current exposure) plus an add-on for potential future exposure.[1]

TECHNOLOGY

Advances in computer systems and related advances in information technology—such as the development of historic loan databases by the Loan Pricing Corporation and other companies—have given banks and FIs the opportunity to test high-powered modeling techniques. For example, besides being able to analyze loan loss and value distribution functions and (especially) the tails of such distributions, they can move toward actively managing loan portfolios based on modern portfolio theory (MPT) models and techniques.[2]

THE BIS RISK-BASED CAPITAL REQUIREMENTS

Despite the importance of the six reasons discussed above, probably the greatest incentive for banks to develop new credit risk models has been dissatisfaction with the BIS and central banks'

---

[1] See the discussion in Saunders (1997), and Chapter 13.

[2] Arguably, technology and the increased liquidity in the secondary market for loans (along with the development of credit derivatives) have helped move the "lending paradigm" away from a buy-and-hold strategy to one in which loans and credit risk are actively managed in a portfolio framework [see, for example, Kuritzkes (1998)].

post-1992 imposition of capital requirements on loans. The current BIS approach has been described as a "one size fits all" policy; virtually all loans to private-sector counterparties are subjected to the same 8 percent capital ratio (or capital reserve requirement), irrespective of the size of the loan, its maturity, and, most importantly, the credit quality of the borrowing counterparty (see Appendix 1.1). Thus, loans to a firm near bankruptcy are treated (in capital requirement terms) in the same fashion as loans to a AAA borrower. Further, the current capital requirement is additive across all loans; there is no allowance for lower capital requirements because of a greater degree of diversification in the loan portfolio.

At the beginning of 1998 in the United States (1997 in the European Community), regulators allowed certain large banks, the discretion to calculate capital requirements for their trading books—or market risk exposures—using "internal models" rather than the alternative regulatory ("standardized") model. Internal models have had certain constraints imposed on them by regulators and are subjected to back-testing verification;[3] nevertheless, they potentially allow for (1) the value at risk (VAR) of each tradable instrument to be more accurately measured (e.g., based on its price volatility, maturity, etc.) and (2) correlations among assets to be taken into account. In the context of market risk, VAR measures the market value exposure of a financial instrument in case tomorrow is a "bad day," defined statistically. For example, under the BIS market risk regulations, when banks calculate their VAR-based capital requirements using their internal models, they are required to measure the bad day as the 1 bad day that happens once every 100 business days.

The questions for bankers and regulators, and among the major questions analyzed in this book, are:

1. Can an "internal model" approach be used to measure the value at risk or capital exposure of (nontradable) loans?

---

[3] For a discussion, see Lopez and Saidenberg (1998).

2. Do internal models have sufficient flexibility and accuracy to supplant the current standardized 8 percent risk-based capital ratio that imposes the same capital requirement on virtually all private-sector loans?

Even if it is felt that internal models have some way to go before they can replace the 8 percent rule—especially because of the nontradability of loans compared to marketable instruments, and the lack of deep historic databases on loan defaults—the new internal models may still have significant value to bankers, FI risk managers, regulators, and corporate treasurers.[4] Specifically, internal models potentially offer better ways to value outstanding loans and credit-risk-exposed instruments such as bonds (corporate and emerging market), as well as better methods for predicting default risk exposures to borrowers and derivative counterparties. Moreover, internal models (1) allow (in many cases) the credit risk of portfolios of loans and credit-risk-sensitive instruments to be better evaluated, and (2) can be used to improve the pricing of new loans, in the context of an FI's risk-adjusted return on capital (RAROC), and of relatively new instruments in the credit-derivatives markets, such as credit options, credit swaps, and credit forwards. Finally, the models provide an opportunity to measure the privately optimal or economic amount of capital a bank (or FI) should hold as part of its capital structure.

Before we look at some of these new approaches to credit risk measurement, a brief analysis of the more traditional approaches will heighten the contrast between the new and traditional approaches to credit-risk measurement.

---

[4] At the time of this writing, the BIS Committee was about to release a document considering changes to the current credit-risk capital requirement. It is widely expected that a three-stage plan will be suggested. The first stage will involve minor modifications to the BIS rules, the second stage will involve the greater use of bank rating systems, while the third will invoive a potential movement toward the use of bank internal models.

Appendix **1.1**

Risk-Based Capital (RBC) Requirements for Selected Banking Book Instruments

Percent of maximum possible credit loss.

Type of Instrument	Effective Total RBC Requirement
Whole loans:	
Uncollateralized/guaranteed	8.0 percent
Collateralized/guaranteed	
*OECD government	0.0
OECD bank/securities dealer	1.6
Other collateral/guarantee	8.0
Loan commitments:	
One year or less	0.0
More than one year	4.0
Written put options (loans or bonds)	0.0
Financial guarantees (including credit derivatives):	
Direct credit substitute	8.0
Recourse	8.0 to 100 (usually 100 percent under "low-level recourse" rule)

*OECD = Organization for Economic Cooperation and Development.
Source: Federal Reserve Board of Governors.

Chapter 2

Traditional Approaches to Credit Risk Measurement

INTRODUCTION

It is hard to draw the line between traditional and new approaches, especially because many of the better ideas of traditional models are used in the new models. I view three classes of models as comprising the traditional approach: (1) expert systems, (2) rating systems, and (3) credit-scoring systems. For a more complete discussion of these models, see Caouette, Altman, and Narayanan (1998).

EXPERT SYSTEMS

In an expert system, the credit decision is left to the local or branch lending officer. Implicitly, this person's expertise, subjective judgment, and weighting of certain key factors are the most important determinants in the decision to grant credit. The potential factors and expert systems a lending officer could look at are infinite; however, one of the most common expert systems, the five "Cs" of credit, will yield sufficient understanding. The expert analyzes these five key factors, subjectively weights them, and reaches a credit decision:

1. *Character*—a measure of the reputation of the firm, its willingness to repay, and its repayment history. In particular, it has been established empirically that the age of a firm is a good proxy for its repayment reputation.

2. *Capital*—the equity contribution of owners and its ratio to debt (leverage). These are viewed as good predictors of bankruptcy probability. High leverage suggests greater probability of bankruptcy than low leverage.

3. *Capacity*—the ability to repay, which reflects the volatility of the borrower's earnings. If repayments on debt contracts follow a constant stream over time, but earnings are volatile (or have a high standard deviation), there may be periods when the firm's capacity to repay debt claims is constrained.

4. *Collateral*—in the event of default, a banker has claims on the collateral pledged by the borrower. The greater the priority of this claim and the greater the market value of the underlying collateral, the lower the exposure risk of the loan.

5. *Cycle or (Economic) Conditions*—the state of the business cycle; an important element in determining credit risk exposure, especially for cycle-dependent industries. For example, durable goods sectors tend to be more cycle-dependent than nondurable goods sectors. Similarly, industries that have exposure to international competitive conditions tend to be cycle-sensitive. Taylor (1998), in an analysis of Dun and Bradstreet bankruptcy data by industry (both means and standard deviations), found some quite dramatic differences in U.S. industry failure rates during the business cycle.

In addition to these five "Cs," an expert might take into account the level of interest rates. As is well known from economic theory, the relationship between the level of interest rates and the expected return on a loan is highly nonlinear [see Stiglitz and Weiss (1981)]. At "low" levels of interest rates, the expected return could increase if rates are raised. However, at "high" levels of interest rates, an increase in rates may lower the return on a loan. This negative relationship between high loan rates and expected loan returns is due to two effects: (1) adverse selection and (2) risk shifting. When loan rates rise beyond some point, good borrowers drop out of the loan market, preferring to self-finance their investment projects (adverse selection). The remaining borrowers, who have limited liability and limited equity at stake, have the incentive to shift into riskier projects (risk shifting). In good times, they will be able to repay the bank. If times turn bad and they default, they will have limited downside loss.

Although many banks still use expert systems as part of their credit decision process, these systems face two main problems:

1. Consistency: What are the important common factors to analyze across different types of borrower?
2. Subjectivity: What are the optimal weights to apply to the factors chosen?

Potentially, the subjective weights applied to the five Cs by an expert can vary from borrower to borrower if the expert so chooses. This makes comparability of rankings and decisions very difficult for an individual monitoring an expert's decision and for other experts in general. As a result, quite different standards can be applied by credit officers, within any given bank or FI, to similar types of borrower. It can be argued that loan committees or multilayered signature authorities are key mechanisms in avoiding such consistency problems, but it is unclear how effectively they impose common standards in practice.[1]

---

[1] Treacy and Carey (1998) argue that loan review departments are further mechanisms through which common standards can be applied across lending officers.

RATING SYSTEMS

One of the oldest rating systems for loans was developed by the U.S. Office of the Comptroller of the Currency (OCC). The system has been used in the United States (and abroad) by regulators and bankers to assess the adequacy of their loan loss reserves. The OCC rating system places an existing loan portfolio into five categories: four low-quality ratings and one high-quality rating. In the list below, the required loss reserve appears next to each category:

Loss Reserves

Low-quality ratings:

Other assets especially mentioned (OAEM)	0%
Substandard assets	20
Doubtful assets	50
Loss assets	100

High-quality rating:

Pass/performing	0^2

Over the years, bankers have extended the OCC rating system by developing internal rating systems that more finely subdivide the pass/performing rating category. For example, at any given moment, there is always a chance that some pass or performing loans will go into default, and that some reserves, even if very low (e.g., 0.2 percent), should be held against these loans. Currently, it is estimated that about 60 percent of U.S. bank holding companies have developed internal rating systems for loans on a 1–9 or 1–10 scale [see Fadil (1997)], including the top 50 [Treacy & Carey

---

[2] Technically speaking, the 0 percent loss reserves for OAEM and pass loans are lower bounds. In practice, the reserve rates on these categories are determined by the bank in consultation with examiners, depending on some type of "historical analysis" of charge-off rates for the bank.

(1998)].[3] An example of a 1–10 loan rating system and its mapping into equivalent bond ratings is shown in Table 2.1.

The OCC pass grade is divided into six different categories (ratings 1–6). Ratings 7–10 correspond to the OCC's four low-quality loan ratings. These loan-rating systems do not exactly map into bond rating systems, especially at the lower-quality end. One reason is that loan-rating systems are supposed to rate an individual loan (including its covenants and collateral backing); bond rating systems are more oriented to rating the overall borrower. This lack of one-to-one mapping between bond ratings and loan ratings raises a flag as to the merits of those newer models that rely on bond data (spreads, transition matrixes, and so on) to value and to price loans.

Given this trend toward finer internal ratings of loans, compared to the OCC's regulatory model, the Federal Reserve System Task Force Report (1998) and Mingo (1998) give some tentative support for using an internal model "ratings-based" approach as an alternative to the OCC model, to calculate capital reserves against unexpected losses, and loan loss reserves against expected loan losses. For example, using the outstanding dollar value of loans in each internal rating class (1–10), a bank might calculate its capital requirement against unexpected loan losses as follows:

Capital
requirement = [Total loans in rating class 1 × 0.2 percent]
+
•
•
•
+
[Total loans in rating class 10 × 100 percent]

---

[3] Smaller banking organizations tend to have fewer grades on their scales, or no rating systems at all.

Table 2.1   An Example of a Loan Rating System and Bond Rating Mapping

Bond Rating	Score	Risk Level	Description
AAA	1	Minimal	Excellent business credit, superior asset quality, excellent debt capacity and coverage; excellent management with depth. Company is a market leader and has access to capital markets.
AA	2	Modest	Good business credit, very good asset quality and liquidity, strong debt capacity and coverage, very good management in all positions. Company is highly regarded in industry and has a very strong market share.
A	3	Average	Average business credit, within normal credit standards: satisfactory asset quality and liquidity, good debt capacity and coverage; good management in all critical positions. Company is of average size and position within the industry.
BBB	4	Acceptable	Acceptable business credit, but with more than average risk: acceptable asset quality, little excess liquidity, modest debt capacity. May be highly or fully leveraged. Requires above-average levels of supervision and attention from lender. Company is not strong enough to sustain major setbacks. Loans are highly leveraged transactions due to regulatory constraints.
BB	5	Acceptable with care	Acceptable business credit, but with considerable risk: acceptable asset quality, smaller and/or less diverse asset base, very little liquidity, limited debt capacity.

Table 2.1 (Continued)

Bond Rating	Score	Risk Level	Description
			Covenants structured to ensure adequate protection. May be highly or fully leveraged. May be of below-average size or a lower-tier competitor. Requires significant supervision and attention from lender. Company is not strong enough to sustain major setbacks. Loans are highly leveraged transactions due to the obligor's financial status.
B	6	Management attention	Watch list credit: generally acceptable asset quality, somewhat strained liquidity, fully leveraged. Some management weakness. Requires continual supervision and attention from lender.
CCC	7	Special mention (OAEM)	Marginally acceptable business credit; some weakness. Generally undesirable business constituting an undue and unwarranted credit risk but not to the point of justifying a substandard classification. Although the asset is currently protected, it is potentially weak. No loss of principal or interest is envisioned. Potential weaknesses might include a weakening financial condition; an unrealistic repayment program; inadequate sources of funds, or lack of adequate collateral, credit information, or documentation. Company is undistinguished and mediocre.
CCC	8	Substandard	Unacceptable business credit; normal repayment in jeopardy. Although no loss of principal or interest is envisioned, a positive

(continued)

Table 2.1   (Continued)

Bond Rating	Score	Risk Level	Description
			and well-defined weakness jeopardizes collection of debt. The asset is inadequately protected by the current sound net worth and paying capacity of the obligor or pledged collateral. There may already have been a partial loss of interest.
CC/C	9	Doubtful	Full repayment questionable. Serious problems exist to the point where a partial loss of principal is likely. Weaknesses are so pronounced that, on the basis of current information, conditions, and values, collection in full is highly improbable.
D	10	Loss	Expected total loss. An uncollectible asset or one of such little value that it does not warrant classification as an active asset. Such an asset may, however, have recovery or salvage value, but not to the point where a write-off should be deferred, even though a partial recovery may occur in the future.

The 0.2 percent for rating class 1 is just suggestive of unexpected loss rates and should be based on historic loss probabilities of a loan in class 1 moving to class 10 (loss) over the next year.[4] However, an important problem remains, similar to the current 8 percent risk-based capital ratio: No account is taken of

---

[4] To calculate the loan loss reserve against expected losses, a similar approach would be used except that expected loss rates would replace unexpected loss rates.

loan portfolio diversification. The credit risk of each rating class is simply added up to derive a total (dollar) capital requirement.

A second, and related, use for internal ratings has been suggested by Fadil (1997). Calculate a weighted-average risk rating (WARR) based on the loans allocated to each of the rating classes:

$$\mathrm{WARR} = \sum_{i=1}^{n} r_i x e_i \Big/ \sum_{i=1}^{n} e_i$$

where: r_i = risk rating class ($i = 1, \ldots n$)
  e_i = loan exposure in that class.

Fadil (1997) suggests a weighting system based on the proportion of unexpected losses in each class. Using the type of models discussed in Chapters 3 through 8, calculate an "unexpected loss rate" for a typical loan in each rating class, and employ these loss rates as the appropriate weighting system in calculating an aggregate WARR for a bank. The WARR might be tracked over time and compared with peer banks.[5]

CREDIT SCORING SYSTEMS

Credit scoring systems can be found in virtually all types of credit analysis, from consumer credit to commercial loans. The idea is essentially the same: Pre-identify certain key factors that determine the probability of default (as opposed to repayment), and combine or weight them into a quantitative score. In some cases, the score can be literally interpreted as a probability of default; in others, the score can be used as a classification system: it places a potential borrower into either a good or a bad group, based on a score and a cutoff point. Full reviews of the traditional approach

---

[5] Although the concerns regarding portfolio aspects and loan decision making aspects of rating models remain.

to credit scoring, and the various methodologies, can be found in Caouette, Altman, and Narayanan (1998) and Saunders (1997). A good review of the worldwide application of credit-scoring models can be found in Altman and Narayanan (1997).

Because this book is concerned with newer models of credit risk measurement, one simple example of this type of model will suffice to bring up some of the issues supposedly addressed by many of the newer models.

Consider the Altman (1968) Z-score model, which is a classificatory model for corporate borrowers (but can also be used to get a default probability prediction). Based on a matched sample (by year, size, and industry) of failed and solvent firms, and using linear discriminant analysis, the best fitting scoring model for commercial loans took the form:

$$Z = 1.2\ X_1 + 1.4\ X_2 + 3.3\ X_3 + 0.6\ X_4 + 1.0\ X_5$$

where X_1 = working capital/total assets ratio;
X_2 = retained earnings/total assets ratio;
X_3 = earnings before interest and taxes/total assets ratio;
X_4 = market value of equity/book value of total liabilities ratio;
X_5 = sales/total assets ratio.

As used by the credit officer, if a corporate borrower's accounting ratios (the X_i's), when weighted by the estimated coefficients in the Z function, results in a Z score below a critical value (in Altman's initial study, 1.81), they would be classified as "bad" and the loan would be refused.

A number of issues need to be raised here. First, the model is linear whereas the path to bankruptcy may be highly nonlinear (the relationship between the X_i's is likely to be nonlinear as well). Second, with the exception of the market value of equity term in the leverage ratio, the model is essentially based on accounting ratios. In most countries, accounting data appear only at discrete intervals (e.g., quarterly) and are generally based on historic or book value accounting principles. It is also questionable whether such models can pick up a firm whose condition is rapidly deteriorating (e.g., as in the recent Asian crisis). Indeed, as the world becomes more complex and competitive, the predictability of simple Z-score models may worsen. A good example is Brazil. When fitted in the mid-1970s the Z-score model did a quite good job of predicting default even two or three years prior to bankruptcy [Altman, Baidya, and Dias (1977)]. However, more recently, even with low inflation and greater economic stability, this type of model has performed less well as the Brazilian economy has become more open [Sanvicente and Bader (1996)].

Arguably, the recent application of nonlinear methods such as neural networks to credit risk analysis shows promise of improving on the older vintage credit-scoring models. Rather than assuming there is only a linear and direct effect from the X_i variables on Z (the credit score), or, in the language of neural networks, from the input layer to the output layer, neural networks allow for additional explanatory power via complex correlations or interactions among the X_i variables (many of which are nonlinear). Thus, for example, the five variables in the Altman Z-score model can be augmented by some nonlinearly transformed sum of X_1 and X_2 as a further explanatory variable. A good example of an extension of the Altman Z-score model in this direction is offered by Coates and Fant (1993). In neural network terminology the complex correlations among the X_i variables form a "hidden layer" which, when exploited (i.e., included in the model), can improve the fit and reduce type 1 and type 2 errors.[6]

Yet, neural networks pose many problems to financial economists. How many additional hidden correlations should be included? In the language of neural networks, when should training stop? It is entirely possible that a large neural network, including large N nonlinear transformations of sums of the X_i

---

[6] A type 1 error is misclassifying a bad loan as good. A type 2 error is misclassifying a good loan as bad.

variables, can reduce type 1 and type 2 errors of a historic loan database close to zero. However, as is well known, this creates the problem of "overfitting": a model that explains well in-sample may perform quite poorly in predicting out-of-sample. More generally, the issue is: When does one stop adding variables—when the remaining error is reduced to 10 percent, 5 percent, or less? What is thought to be a global minimum forecast error may turn out to be just a local minimum. Finally, the issue of economic meaning is probably what troubles financial economists the most. For example, what is the economic meaning of an exponentially transformed sum of the leverage ratio and the sales-to-total-assets ratio? The ad hoc economic nature of these models and their tenuous links to existing financial theory separate them from some of the newer models that will be discussed in Chapters 3 through 8.

Chapter 3

Loans as Options and the KMV Model

INTRODUCTION

The idea of applying option pricing theory to the valuation of risky loans and bonds has been in the literature at least as far back as Merton (1974). In recent years, Merton's ideas have been extended in many directions. One example is the generation, by the KMV Corporation of San Francisco, of a default prediction model (the Credit Monitor Model) that produces (and updates) default predictions for all major companies and banks that have their equity publicly traded. In this chapter, we first look at the link between loans and options and then investigate how this link can be used to derive a default prediction model.

THE LINK BETWEEN LOANS AND OPTIONALITY

Figure 3.1 shows the payoff function to a bank lender of a simple loan. Assume that this is a one-year loan and the amount 0B is borrowed on a discount basis. Technically, option formulas (discussed later) model loans as zero-coupon "bonds" with fixed maturities. Over the year, the borrowing firm will invest the funds in various projects or assets. Assume that at the end of the year the market value of the borrowing firm's assets is $0A_2$. The owners of the firm have an incentive to repay the loan (0B) and keep the residual as "profit" or return on investment ($0A_2 - 0B$). Indeed,

Figure 3.1   The Payoff to a Bank Lender

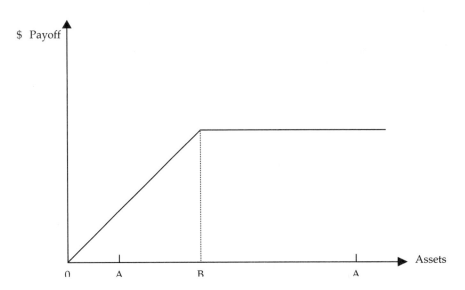

for any value of the firm's assets exceeding 0B, the owners of the firm will have an incentive to repay the loan. However, if the market value of the firm's assets is less than 0B (e.g., $0A_1$ in Figure 3.1), the owners have an incentive (or option) to default and to turn over the remaining assets of the firm to the lender (the bank).

For market values of assets exceeding 0B, the bank will earn a fixed upside return on the loan; essentially, interest and principal will be repaid in full. For asset values less than 0B, the bank suffers increasingly large losses. In the extreme case, the bank's payoff is zero: principal and interest are totally lost.[1]

The loan payoff function shown in Figure 3.1—a fixed payoff on the upside, and long-tailed downside risk—might be immediately familiar to an option theorist. Compare it with the payoff to a

---

[1] In fact, if there are direct and indirect costs of bankruptcy (e.g., legal costs), the lenders loss on a loan may exceed principal and interest. This makes the payoff in Figure 3.1 even more similar to that shown in Figure 3.2 on the next page (i.e., the loan may have a negative dollar payoff).

Figure 3.2   The Payoff to the Writer of a Put Option on a Stock

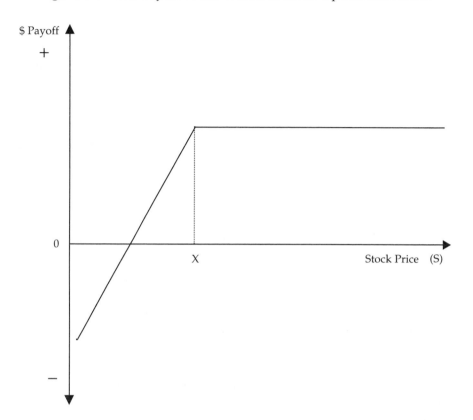

writer of a put option on a stock, shown in Figure 3.2. If the price of the stock *(S)* exceeds the exercise price *(X)*, the writer of the option will keep the put premium. If the price of the stock falls below *X*, the writer will lose successively large amounts.

Merton (1974) noted this formal payoff equivalence; that is, when a bank makes a loan, its payoff is isomorphic to writing a put option on the assets of the borrowing firm. Moreover, just as five variables enter the classic Black–Scholes–Merton (BSM) model of put option valuation for stocks, the value of the default option (or, more generally, the value of a risky loan) will also depend on the value of five similar variables.

In general form:

$$\text{Value of a put option on a stock} = f\left(\overline{S}, \overline{X}, \overline{r}, \sigma_s, \overline{\tau}\right) \quad (3.1)$$

$$\text{Value of a default option on a risky loan} = f\left(A, \overline{B}, \overline{r}, \sigma_A, \overline{\tau}\right) \quad (3.2)$$

where S, X, A, and B are as defined above (a bar above a variable denotes that it is directly observable); r is the short-term interest rate; σ_s and σ_A are, respectively, the volatilities of the firm's equity value and the market value of its assets; and τ is the maturity of the put option or, in the case of loans, the time horizon (default horizon) for the loan.

In general, for options on stocks, all five variables on the right-hand side (RHS) of equation (3.1) are directly observable; however, this is true for only three variables on the RHS of equation (3.2). The market value of a firm's assets (A) and the volatility of the market value of a firm's assets (σ_A) are not directly observable. If A and σ_A could be directly measured, the value of a risky loan, the value of the default option, and the equilibrium spread on a risky loan over the risk-free rate could all be calculated. [See Merton (1974) and Saunders (1997) for examples; see also the appendix to this chapter.]

Some analysts have substituted the observed market value of risky debt on the left-hand side (LHS) of equation (3.2) (or, where appropriate, the observed interest spread between a firm's risky bonds and a matched risk-free Treasury rate) and have assumed that the book value of assets equals the market value of assets. This allows the implied volatility of assets (σ_A) to be "backed out" from equation (3.2). [See, for example, Gorton and Santomero (1990) and Flannery and Sorescu (1996).] However, without additional assumptions, it is impossible to impute two unobservable values (A and σ_A), based solely on one equation (3.2). Moreover, the market value of risky corporate debt is hard to get for all but a few firms. Corporate bond price information is generally not easily available to the public, and quoted bond prices are often artificial "matrix" prices.[2, 3]

THE KMV CREDIT MONITOR MODEL[4]

The innovation of the KMV Credit Monitor Model is that it turns the bank's lending problem around and considers the loan repayment incentive problem from the viewpoint of the borrowing firm's equity holders. To solve the two unknowns, A and σ_A, the model uses (1) the "structural" relationship between the market value of a firm's equity and the market value of its assets, and (2) the relationship between the volatility of a firm's assets and the volatility of a firm's equity. After values of these variables are derived, an expected default frequency (EDF) measure for the borrower can be calculated.

Figure 3.3 shows the loan repayment problem from the side of the borrower (the equity owner of the firm). Suppose the firm borrows 0B and the end-of-period market value of the firm's assets is $0A_2$ (where $0A_2 > 0B$). The firm will then repay the loan, and the equity owners will keep the residual value of the firm's assets ($0A_2 - 0B$). The larger the market value of the firm's assets at the end of the loan period, the greater the residual value of the firm's assets

---

[2] Specifically, most corporate bonds are traded over-the-counter. Price information is extremely difficult to get because most trades are interdealer. In September 1998, the Securities and Exchange Commission (SEC) announced a special joint initiative with the National Association of Securities Dealers (NASD), to improve the quality of corporate bond price information over the next two years.

[3] Jarrow and van Deventer (1999) have tested a Merton-type model using bond quotes (spreads) for one bank (Interstate Bankcorp) over the January 3, 1986, to August 20, 1993, period. They find considerable instability in implied default probabilities. This may, in part, be due to the use of bond quotes rather than transaction prices. See also, Saunders, Srinivasan, and Walter (1998) for a discussion of price formation in OTC corporate bond markets.

[4] See the Bibliography for references to KMV publications.

Figure 3.3 Equity as a Call Option on a Firm

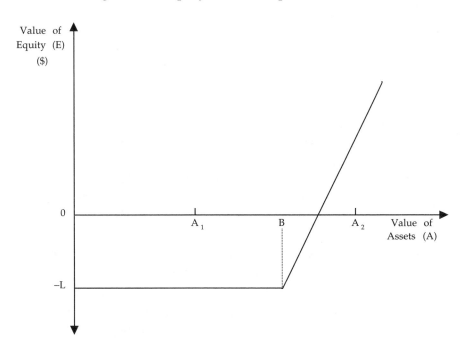

to the equity holders. However, if the firm's assets fall below 0B (e.g., are equal to $0A_1$), the equity owners of the firm will not be able to repay the loan.[5] They will be economically insolvent and will turn the firm's assets over to the bank. Note that the downside risk of the equity owners is truncated no matter how low asset values are, compared to the amount borrowed. Specifically, "limited liability" protects the equity owners against losing more than 0L (the owners' original stake in the firm). As shown in Figure 3.3, the payoff to the equity holder of a leveraged firm has a limited downside and a long-tailed upside. Those familiar with options will immediately recognize the similarity between the payoff function of

---

[5] For example, if the assets are liquidated at current market values and the resulting funds are used to meet borrowing obligations.

an equity owner in a leveraged firm and buying a call option on a stock. Thus, we can view the market-value position of equity holders in a borrowing firm (E) as isomorphic to holding a call option on the assets of the firm (A).

In general terms; equity can be valued as:

$$\overline{E} = h\left(A, \sigma_A, \overline{r}, \overline{B}, \overline{\tau}\right) \tag{3.3}$$

In equation (3.3), the observed market value of a borrowing firm's equity (price of shares × number of shares) depends on the same five variables as in equation (3.2), as per the BSM model for valuing a call option (on the assets of a firm). However, a problem still remains: how to solve two unknowns (A and σ_A) from one equation (where E, r, B, and τ are all observable, as denoted by the bar above them).

KMV and others in the literature have resolved this problem by noting that a second relationship can be exploited: the theoretical relationship between the observable volatility of a firm's equity value (σ_E) and the "unobservable" volatility of a firm's asset value (σ_A). In general terms:

$$\overline{\sigma}_E = g\left(\sigma_A\right) \tag{3.4}$$

With two equations and two unknowns, equations (3.3) and (3.4) can be used to solve for A and σ_A by successive iteration. Explicit functional forms for the option-pricing model (OPM) in equation (3.3) and for the stock price–asset volatility linkage in equation (3.4) have to be specified. [A good discussion of these issues can be found in Jarrow and Turnbull (1998) and Delianedis and Geske (1998).] KMV use an option-pricing BSM-type model that allows for dividends. B, the default exercise point, is taken as the value of all short-term liabilities (one year and under) plus half the book value of long-term debt outstanding. (The precise strike price "or default boundary" has varied

Figure 3.4   Calculating the Theoretical EDF

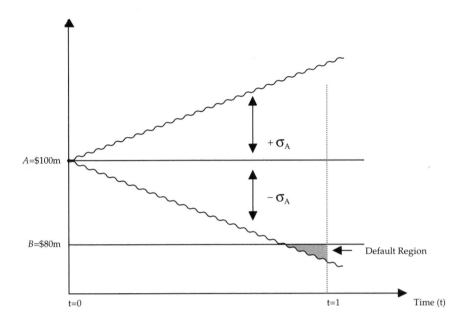

under different generations of the model, and there is a question as to whether net short-term liabilities should be used instead of total short-term liabilities.[6]) The maturity variable (τ) also can be altered according to the default horizon of the analyst; most commonly, it is set equal to one year. A slightly different OPM was used by Ronn and Verma (1986, p. 878) to solve a very similar problem estimating the default risk of U.S. banks.

After they have been calculated, the A and σ_A values can be employed, along with assumptions about the values of B and τ, to generate a theoretically based EDF score for any given borrower.

The idea is shown in Figure 3.4. Suppose that the values backed out of equations (3.3) and (3.4) for any given borrower are,

---

[6] KMV also doesn't make distinctions in the liability structure as to seniority, collateral, or covenants. Also, convertible debt and preferred stock are treated as long-term liabilities. It might be noted, however, that the user can input whatever value of B he or she feels is economically appropriate.

respectively: A = $100 million and σ_A = $10 million.[7] The value of B = $80 million. In practice, the user can set the default boundary or "exercise price" (B) equal to any proportion of total debt outstanding that is of interest. Suppose we want to calculate the EDF for a one-year horizon. Given the values of A, σ_A, B, and r, and with τ = one year, what is the (theoretical) probability of a borrowing firm's failure at the one-year horizon? As can be seen in Figure 3.4, the EDF is the cross-hatched area of the distribution of asset values below B. This area represents the probability that the current value of the firm's assets, $100 million, will drop below $80 million at the one-year time horizon.

If it is assumed that future asset values are normally distributed around the firm's current asset value, we can measure the $t = 0$ (or today's) distance from default at the one-year horizon as:

$$\text{Distance from default} = \frac{A - B}{\sigma_A} = \frac{\$100\text{m} - \$80\text{m}}{\$10\text{m}} \qquad (3.5)$$

$$= 2 \text{ standard deviations}$$

For the firm to enter the default region (the cross-hatched area), asset values would have to drop by $20 million, or 2 standard deviations, during the next year. If asset values are normally distributed, we know that there is a 95 percent probability that asset values will vary between plus and minus 2σ from their mean value. Thus, there is a 2½ percent probability that asset values will increase by more than 2σ over the next year, and a 2½ percent probability that they will fall by more than 2σ. In other words, there is an expected default frequency or EDF of 2½ percent. We have shown no growth in expected or mean asset values over the one-year period in Figure 3.4, but this can easily be incorporated. For example, if we project that the value of the firm's assets will grow 10 percent over the next year, then the relevant EDF would be lower because asset values would have to drop by

---

[7] Where σ_A is the annual standard deviation of asset values.

3σ, which is below the firm's expected asset growth path, for the firm to default at year-end.[8]

The idea of asset values normally distributed around some mean level plays a crucial role in calculating joint default transition probabilities in J.P. Morgan's CreditMetrics (see Chapter 4), yet there is an important issue as to whether it is (theoretically or empirically) reasonable to make this assumption. With this in mind, rather than producing theoretical EDFs, the KMV approach generates an empirical EDF along the following lines. Suppose that we have a large historic database of firm defaults and no defaults (repayments), and we calculate that the firm we are analyzing has a theoretical distance from default of 2σ. We then ask the empirical question: What percentage of firms in the database actually defaulted within the one-year time horizon when their asset values placed them a distance of 2σ away from default at the beginning of the year, and how does that compare to the total population of firms that were 2σ away from default at the beginning of the year? This produces an empirical EDF:

$$\text{Empirical EDF} = \frac{\begin{array}{c}\text{Number of firms that defaulted within} \\ \text{a year with asset values of } 2\sigma \text{ from} \\ B \text{ at the beginning of the year}\end{array}}{\begin{array}{c}\text{Total population of firms with} \\ \text{asset values of } 2\sigma \text{ from } B \\ \text{at the beginning of the year}\end{array}}$$

---

[8] Distance from default $= \dfrac{A(1+g)-B}{\sigma_A} = \dfrac{\$110-\$80}{\$10} = 3$ standard deviations.

KMV Credit Monitor uses a constant asset growth assumption for all firms in the same market, which is the expected growth rate of the market as a whole. The rationale for this assumption is that in an efficient market, differences in growth rates between the market and individual firms are fully discounted (i.e., arbitraged away) and incorporated in the stock prices (and hence to asset value) of the firm. Thus in equilibrium, there is no difference between asset growth of individual firms and the market. The only other adjustment to this constant (across-the-board) asset growth rate is for firm-specific payouts such as dividends or interest payment. The adjusted number is then applied to the implied current asset value in the distance to default formula.

Suppose, based on a worldwide database, it was estimated that 50 of 1,000 possible firms defaulted. The equation would be:

$$\text{Empirical EDF} = \frac{50\,\text{Defaults}}{1{,}000\text{- Firm population}} = 5\,\text{percent}$$

As a result, this empirically based EDF can differ quite significantly from the theoretically based EDF. From a proprietary perspective, KMV's advantage comes from building up a large worldwide database of firms (and firm defaults) that can produce such empirically based EDF scores.

A question arises as to how EDF scores perform relative to accounting-based scores and rating systems. Figure 3.5 shows the

Figure 3.5 KMV Expected Default Frequency™ and Agency Rating for IBM

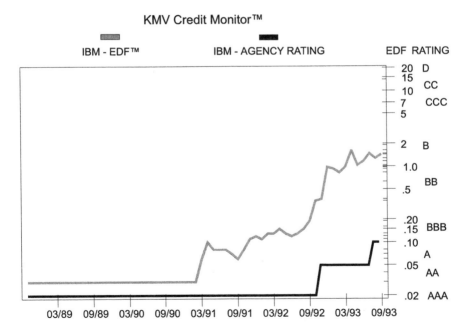

Source: CREDIT MONITOR™, KMV CORPORATION © 1993.

KMV-produced EDF scores for IBM over a five-year period (using a log-scale) when IBM's credit quality deteriorated. Note that EDF scores vary between 0 and 20 percent. The EDF of IBM started to rise well before the deterioration in its agency rating. Figure 3.6 shows a more recent Asian example, the EDF scores of Krung Thai Bank from June 1993 to December 1997. The EDF for the bank was rising well before the genesis of the Thai crisis in mid-1997. This greater sensitivity of EDF scores, compared to both accounting-based and rating-based systems, comes from the direct link between EDF scores and stock market prices. As new information about a borrower is generated, its stock price and stock price volatility will react, as will its implied asset value (A)

Figure 3.6   KMV Expected Default Frequency™ and
Agency Rating for Krung Thai Bank

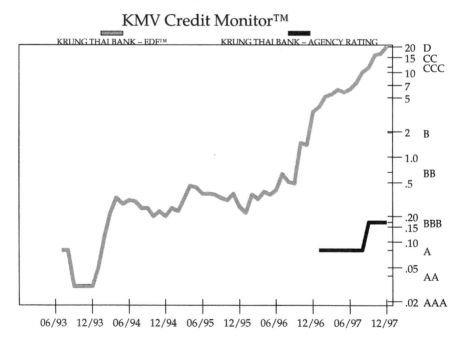

Source: CREDIT MONITOR™, KMV CORPORATION © 1997.

and standard deviation of asset value (σ_A).[9] Changes in A and σ_A generate changes in EDFs. For actively traded firms, it would be possible, in theory, to update an EDF every few minutes. In actuality, KMV can update EDF scores frequently (in many cases, monthly) for some 20,000 firms worldwide.

Because an EDF score reflects information signals transmitted from equity markets, it might be argued that the model is likely to work best in highly efficient equity market conditions and might not work well in many emerging markets. This argument ignores the fact that many thinly traded stocks are those of relatively closely held companies. Thus, major trades by "insiders," such as sales of large blocks of shares (and thus, major movements in a firm's stock price), may carry powerful informational signals about the future prospects of a borrowing firm.[10]

In sum, the option pricing approach to bankruptcy prediction has a number of strengths. First, it can be applied to any public company. Second, by being based on stock market data rather than "historic" book value accounting data, it is forward-looking. Third, it has strong theoretical underpinnings; because it is a "structural model" based on the modern theory of corporate finance and options, where equity is viewed as a call option on the assets of a firm.

---

[9] Another reason for the better predictability of KMV scores over the short horizon is that Standard and Poor's and Moody's calibrate their rating to default experience over the past 20-plus years. Their probabilities therefore reflect a "cycle average" view. By comparison, KMV's EDFs reflect strong cyclicality over the business cycle. Some studies have shown that EDFs do not offer any advantage for time horizons over two years; see Miller (1998). KMV also argues that using their model reduces actual defaults by a greater amount than agency ratings such as S&P. Specifically, KMV uses a power curve analysis where loan applicants are sorted by EDF and S&P ratings. If the worst credits, say the bottom 30%, are outrightly rejected, then among the ones that are funded about 90% of defaults are avoided under the EDF scheme, versus 70% under the S&P scheme.

[10] For example, an insider might sell a large block if he or she has private information about the adverse nature of future prospects for the firm.

Against these strengths are four weaknesses: (1) it is difficult to construct theoretical EDFs without the assumption of normality of asset returns; (2) private firms' EDFs can be calculated only by using some comparability analysis based on accounting data and other observable characteristics of the borrower; (3) it does not distinguish among different types of long-term bonds according to their seniority, collateral, covenants, or convertibility; and (4) it is "static" in that the Merton model assumes that once management puts a debt structure in place, it leaves it unchanged—even if the value of a firm's assets has doubled. As a result, the Merton model cannot capture the behavior of those firms that seek to maintain a constant or target leverage ratio across time [see Jarrow & van Deventer (1999)].

STRUCTURAL MODELS AND INTENSITY-BASED MODELS

A further potential problem with KMV-type models, and the BSM structural model approach on which it is based, are the implications for the probability of default and credit spreads as the time to default, or the maturity of debt, shrinks. Under normal BSM continuous time diffusion processes for asset values, the probability that a firm's asset value (A) will fall below its debt boundary (B) (Figure 3.4) declines dramatically as the default horizon (τ) goes to zero. Indeed, the implication of structural models is that the credit spread at the very short end of the risky debt market should be zero. [See Leland (1994), for example.]

In general, however, observable short-term credit spreads are nonzero. It could be argued that this is due to liquidity and transaction cost effects, but there is a conflicting opinion that the structural models of the BSM (and KMV) type—and especially the underlying assumptions of these models, regarding the diffusion of asset values over time (see Figure 3.4)—underestimate the probability of default over short horizons.[11] Not surprisingly, considerable recent research has focused on resolving this issue by modifying

---

[11] See, for example, Jones, Mason, and Rosenfeld (1984).

the basic assumptions of the BSM model. The work by Zhou (1997) attempts to address underestimation of short-horizon risk by allowing for jumps in the asset value *(A)* of the firm. Related work by Jarrow and Turnbull (1998) and Duffie and Singleton (1998), on "intensity-based" models, presents an alternative approach to resolving the short-term horizon problem. Intensity-based models apply fixed or variable hazard functions to default risk. Essentially, rather than assuming a structural model of default (as in the BSM approach), in which a firm defaults when asset values fall below debt values, the intensity-based model is a "reduced-form" model; default follows a Poisson distribution, and default arises contingent on the arrival of some "hazard."[12] Duffie and Lando (1997) have sought to integrate the intensity-based approach into the structural approach. Suppose that asset values in the context of the structural model are noisy in that they cannot be perfectly observed by outsiders. In this context, accounting information releases may partially resolve this information gap and lead to jumps in asset values as investors revise their expectations. Thus, imperfect information and fuzziness in observed asset values may potentially be integrated into the OPM (structural) framework and resolve the underestimation of default risk at the short horizon. Work by Leland (1994), by Anderson, Sunderesan, and Tychon (1996), and by Mella-Barral and Perraudin (1997), which extends the BSM model by allowing for debt renegotiations (i.e., renegotiations of the debt boundary value, or *B*), can be thought of as work in a similar spirit,[13] as can that of Leland (1998), who builds in agency costs as a friction to the traditional BSM model and Acharya and Carpenter (1999) who model callable defautable bonds under conditions of stochastic interest rates and endogenous bankruptcy.

---

[12] See, also, Duffee (1999) for a review of intensity-based models.

[13] For example, the boundary will become stochastic if there is liquidation cost to asset values. This gives firms power to renegotiate. In Merton's (1974) original model, there are no costs to liquidation, *i.e.*, assets are liquidated and paid out costlessly. [See also Longstaff and Schwartz (1995).]

Appendix **3.1**

Merton's Valuation Model

The equation for the market value of risky debt, $F(\tau)$, takes the form:

$$F(\tau) = Be^{-i\tau} [(1/d) N (h_1) + N(h_2)] \qquad (A.1)$$

where $\tau =$ the length of time remaining to loan maturity; that is, $\tau = T - t$, where T is the maturity date, and t is current time (today).

$d =$ the firm's (the borrower's) leverage ratio measured as $Be^{-i\tau}/A$, where the market value of debt is valued at the rate i, the risk-free rate of interest.

$N(h) =$ a value computed from the standardized normal distribution statistical tables. This value reflects the probability that a deviation exceeding the calculated value of h will occur.

$$h_1 = -[\tfrac{1}{2} \sigma^2\tau - \ln (d)]/\sigma\sqrt{\tau}$$

$$h_2 = -[\tfrac{1}{2} \sigma^2\tau + \ln (d)]/\sigma\sqrt{\tau}$$

where σ^2 measures the asset risk of the borrower—technically, the variance of the rate of change in the value of the underlying assets of the borrower.

This equation also can be written in terms of a yield spread that reflects an equilibrium default risk-premium that the borrower should be charged:

$$k(\tau) - i = (-1/\tau) \ln [N(h_2) + (1/d) N (h_1)]$$

where $k(\tau)$ = the required yield on risky debt,
  $\ln$ = natural logarithm,
   i = the risk-free rate on debt of equivalent maturity
    (here, one period).

An example:[14]

$$B = \$100,000,$$

$$\tau = 1 \text{ year,}$$

$$i = 5 \text{ percent,}$$

$$d = 90 \text{ percent or } .9,$$

$$\sigma = 12 \text{ percent.}$$

Substituting these values into the equations for h_1 and h_2, and solving for the areas under the standardized normal distribution, we find:

$$N(h_1) = .174120$$

$$N(h_2) = .793323$$

$$\text{where } h_1 = \frac{-\left[\frac{1}{2}(.12)^2 + \ln(.9)\right]}{.12} = -.938$$

and

$$h_2 = \frac{-\left[\frac{1}{2}(.12)^2 - \ln(.9)\right]}{.12} = +.818$$

---

[14] This is based on Babbel (1989).

Thus, the current market value of the risky $100,000 loan (L) is:

$$L(t) = Be^{-it}\left[N(h_2) + (1/d)N(h_1)\right]$$

$$= \frac{\$100,000}{1.05127}\left[.793323 + (1.1111)(.17412)\right]$$

$$= \frac{\$100,000}{1.05127}[.986788]$$

$$= \$93,866.18$$

and the required risk spread or premium is:

$$k(\tau) - i = \left(\frac{-1}{\tau}\right)ln\left[N(h_2) + (1/d)N(h_1)\right]$$

$$= (-1)ln[.986788]$$

$$= 1.33 \text{ percent}$$

Chapter 4

The VAR Approach: J.P. Morgan's CreditMetrics and Other Models

INTRODUCTION

Since 1993, when the Bank for International Settlements (BIS) announced its intention to introduce a capital requirement for market risk, great strides have been made in developing and testing methodologies of value at risk (VAR). The incentive to develop internal VAR models was given a further boost in 1995, when the BIS amended its market risk proposal and agreed to allow certain banks to use their own internal models, rather than the standardized model proposed by regulators, to calculate their market risk exposures. Since 1997 in the European Community and 1998 in the United States, the largest banks (subject to regulatory approval) have been able to use their internal models to calculate VAR exposures for the trading book and, thus, capital requirements for market risk.[1]

In this chapter, we first review the basic VAR concept and then look at its potential extension to nontradable loans and its

---

[1] The capital requirements for market risk contain a general market risk component and a specific risk component. For example, with respect to corporate bonds that are held in the trading book, an internal model calculation of specific risk would include features such as spread risk, downgrade risk, and concentration risk. Each of these is related to credit risk. Thus, the 1998 BIS market risk capital requirement contains a credit risk component.

substitution as a model for the 8 percent risk-based capital ratio currently applied when calculating the capital requirement for loans in the banking book. Considerable attention will be paid to CreditMetrics, developed by J.P. Morgan in conjunction with several other sponsors (including KMV). CreditMetrics is nonproprietary and provides a useful benchmark for analyzing the issues and problems of VAR modeling for loans. The VAR approach will be revisited again in Chapter 10 in the context of loan portfolio risk.

THE CONCEPT OF VALUE AT RISK (VAR)

Essentially, VAR models seek to measure the maximum loss (of value) on a given asset or liability over a given time period at a given confidence level (e.g., 95 percent, 97½ percent, 99 percent, etc.).

A simple example of a tradable instrument such as an equity will suffice to describe the basic concept of VAR methodology (see Figure 4.1). Suppose the market price *(P)* of an equity today is $80, and the estimated daily standard deviation of the value (σ) is $10. Because the trading book is managed over a relatively short horizon, a trader or risk manager may ask: "If tomorrow is a 'bad day,' what is my VAR [size of loss in value at some confidence level]?" Assume that the trader is concerned with the value loss on a bad day that occurs, on average, once in every 100 days, and that daily asset values (returns) are "normally" distributed around the current equity value of $80. Statistically speaking, the one bad day has a 1 percent probability of occurring tomorrow. The area under a normal distribution carries information about probabilities. We know that roughly 68 percent of return observations must lie between +1 and −1 standard deviation from the mean; 95 percent of observations lie between +2 and −2 standard deviations from the mean; and 98 percent of observations lie between +2.33 and −2.33 standard deviations from the mean. With respect to the latter, and in terms of dollars, there is a 1 percent

Figure 4.1   The VAR of a Traded Equity

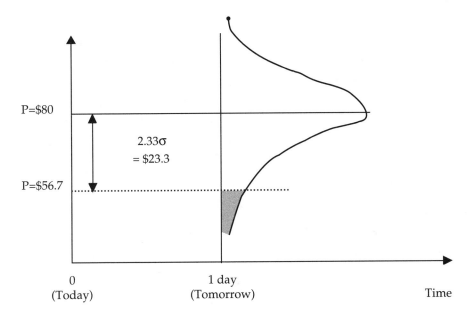

chance that the value of the equity will increase to a value of $80 + 2.33σ tomorrow, and a 1 percent chance it will fall to a value of $80 − 2.33σ. Because σ is assumed to be $10, there is a 1 percent chance that the value of the equity will fall to $56.7 or below; alternatively, there is a 99 percent probability that the equity holder will lose less than $80 − $56.7 = $23.3 in value; that is, $23.3 can be viewed as the VAR on the equity at the 99 percent confidence level. Note that, by implication, there is a 1 percent chance of losing $23.3 *or more* tomorrow. Because, by assumption, asset values are normally distributed, the one bad day in every 100 can lead to the loss being placed anywhere in the shaded region below $56.7 in Figure 4.1. (In reality, losses on non-leveraged financial instruments are truncated at −100 percent of value, and the normal curve is at best an approximation to the log-normal.)

Thus, the key inputs in calculating the VAR of a marketable instrument are its current market value *(P)* and the volatility or standard deviation of that market value (σ). Given an assumed "risk" horizon and a required confidence level (e.g., 99 percent), the VAR can be directly calculated.

Application of this methodology to nontradable loans has some immediate problems. First, P, or the current market value of a loan, is not directly observable because most loans are not traded. Second, because P is not observable, we have no time series to calculate σ, the volatility of P. At best, the assumption of a normal distribution for returns on some tradable assets is a rough approximation, and the approximation becomes even rougher when applied to the possible distribution of values for loans. Specifically, as discussed in Chapter 3, loans have both severely truncated upside returns and long downside risks. As a result, even if we can and do measure P and σ, we still need to take into account the asymmetry of returns on making a loan.

CREDITMETRICS

CreditMetrics was introduced in 1997 by J.P. Morgan and its co-sponsors (Bank of America, KMV, Union Bank of Switzerland, and others) as a value at risk (VAR) framework to apply to the valuation and risk of nontradable assets such as loans and privately placed bonds.[2] RiskMetrics seeks to answer the question: "If tomorrow is a bad day, how much will I lose on tradable assets such as stocks, bonds, and equities?" CreditMetrics asks: "If next year is a bad year, how much will I lose on my loans and loan portfolio?"[3]

As noted above, because loans are not publicly traded, we observe neither P (the loan's market value) nor σ (the volatility of the loan value over the horizon of interest). However, using

---

[2] See CreditMetrics, Technical Document, J.P. Morgan, New York, April 2, 1997. In 1998, the group developing the RiskMetrics and CreditMetrics products formed a separate company called RiskMetrics Group.

[3] The one-year horizon is controversial [see Federal Reserve System Task Force Report (1998)]. For example, if there is some autocorrelation or trend over time toward default, a longer window (say, two years or more) might be appropriate.

(1) available data on a borrower's credit rating, (2) the probability that the rating will change over the next year (the rating transition matrix), (3) recovery rates on defaulted loans, and (4) credit spreads and yields in the bond (or loan) market, it is possible to calculate a hypothetical P and σ for any nontraded loan or bond, and, thus, a VAR figure for individual loans and the loan portfolio.[4]

We will examine, first, a simple example of calculating the VAR on a loan and, second, technical issues surrounding this calculation. Consider, as the example, a five-year fixed-rate loan of $100 million made at 6 percent annual interest.[5] The borrower is rated BBB.

Rating Migration

Based on historical data on publicly-traded bonds (or loans) collected by Standard and Poor's (S&P), Moody's, KMV, or other bond or loan analysts,[6] the probability that a BBB borrower will stay at BBB over the next year is estimated at 86.93 percent. There is also some probability that the borrower will be upgraded (e.g., to A) or will be downgraded (e.g., to CCC or even to default, D). Indeed, eight transitions are possible for the borrower during the next year. Seven involve upgrades, downgrades, and no rating change, and one involves default. The estimated probabilities of these transitions are shown in Table 4.1.[7]

---

[4] As will be discussed in Chapter 10, to calculate the VAR of a loan portfolio we also need to calculate default correlations among counter-parties.

[5] This example is based on the one used in CreditMetrics, Technical Document; see note 2.

[6] As will be discussed later, the choice of transition matrix has a material effect on the VAR calculations. Moreover, the choice of bond transitions to value loans raises again the question of how closely related bonds and loans are.

[7] The rating transitions are based on U.S. corporate bond data. For non-U.S. companies a "mapping" is required for the non-U.S. company into a U.S. company, or else the development of a European or country-specific rating transition matrix is required.

Table 4.1   One-Year Transition Problabilites for BBB-Rated Borrower

AAA	0.02%
AA	0.33
A	5.95
BBB	86.93
BB	5.30
B	1.17
CCC	0.12
Default	0.18

BBB ← Most likely to stay in the same class

Source: CREDITMETRICS-Technical Document, J.P. Morgan, April 2, 1997, p. 11.

Valuation

The effect of rating upgrades and downgrades is to impact the required credit risk spreads or premiums on the loan's remaining cash flows, and, thus, the implied market (or present) value of the loan. If a loan is downgraded, the required credit spread premium should rise (remember that the contractual loan rate in our example is assumed fixed at 6 percent) so that the present value of the loan to the FI should fall. A credit rating upgrade has the opposite effect. Technically, because we are revaluing the five-year, $100 million, 6 percent loan at the end of the first year, after a "credit-event" has occurred during that year, then (measured in millions of dollars):[8]

$$P = 6 + \frac{6}{\left(1 + r_1 + s_1\right)} + \frac{6}{\left(1 + r_2 + s_2\right)^2} + \frac{6}{\left(1 + r_3 + s_3\right)^3} + \frac{106}{\left(1 + r_4 + s_4\right)^4} \quad (4.1)$$

where r_i are the risk-free rates (so called forward zero rates) on zero-coupon T-bonds *expected* to exist one year into the future, and the one-year forward zero rates are calculated from the current

---

[8] Technically, from a valuation perspective the credit-event occurs (by assumption) at the very end of the first year. Currently, CreditMetrics is expanding to allow the credit event "window" to be as short as 3 months or as long as 5 years.

Treasury yield curve (see Appendix 4.1). Further, s_i is the annual credit spread on (zero coupon) loans of a particular rating class of one-year, two-year, three-year, and four-year maturities (the latter are derived from observed spreads in the corporate bond market over Treasuries). In the above example, the first year's coupon or interest payment of $6 million is undiscounted and can be regarded as accrued interest earned on a bond or a loan.

Suppose that, during the first year, the borrower gets upgraded from BBB to A. The present value, or market value, of the loan to the FI at the end of the one-year risk horizon (in millions) is then:[9]

$$P = 6 + \frac{6}{(1.0372)} + \frac{6}{(1.0432)^2} + \frac{6}{(1.0493)^3} + \frac{106}{(1.0532)^4} = \$108.66 \quad (4.2)$$

At the end of the first year, if the loan borrower is upgraded from BBB to A, the $100 million (book value) loan has a market value to the FI of $108.66 million. (This is the value the FI would theoretically be able to obtain at the year-1 horizon if it "sold" the loan in the loan sales market to another FI, at the fair market price or value.) Table 4.2 shows the value of the loan if other credit events occur. Note that the loan has a maximum market value of $109.37 million (if the borrower is upgraded from BBB to AAA) and a minimum value of $51.13 million if the borrower defaults. The latter is the estimated recovery value of the loan [or one minus the loss given default (LGD)] if the borrower declares bankruptcy.[10]

---

[9] In this case, the discount rates reflect the appropriate zero-coupon rates plus credit spreads (s_i) on A-rated loans (bonds). If the borrower's rating were unchanged at BBB, the discount rates would be higher because the credit spreads would reflect the default risk of a BBB borrower. The credit spreads used in CreditMetrics are generated by Bridge and Company, a consulting firm, which updates these rates every week.

[10] Recent studies have suggested that this LGD may be too high for bank loans. A Citibank study of 831 defaulted corporate loans and 89 asset-based loans for 1970–1993 found recovery rates of 79% (or equivalently LGD equal to 21%). Similarly, high recovery rates were found in a Fitch Investor Service report in October 1997 (82%) and a Moody's Investor Service Report of June 1998 (87%). See E. Asarnow (1999).

Table 4.2   Value of the Loan at the End of Year 1, Under Different Ratings (Including First Year Coupon)

Year-End Rating	Value (millions)
AAA	$109.37
AA	109.19
A	108.66
BBB	107.55
BB	102.02
B	98.10
CCC	83.64
Default	51.13

Source: CREDITMETRICS-Technical Document, J.P. Morgan, April 2, 1997, p. 10.

The probability distribution of loan values is shown in Figure 4.2. The value of the loan has a relatively fixed upside and a long downside (i.e., a negative skew). The value of the loan is not symmetrically (or normally) distributed. Thus, CreditMetrics produces two VAR measures:

1. Based on the normal distribution of loan values.
2. Based on the actual distribution of loan values.

Calculation of VAR

Table 4.3 shows the calculation of the VAR, based on each approach, for both the 5 percent and 1 percent worst-case scenarios around the mean or expected (rather than original) loan value. The first step in determining VAR is to calculate the mean of the loan's value, or its expected value, at year 1. This is the sum of each possible loan value, at the end of year 1, times its transition probability over the year. The mean value of the loan is $107.09 (also see Figure 4.2). However, the FI is concerned about unexpected losses or volatility in value. In particular, if next year is

Figure 4.2 Actual Distribution of Loan Values on Five-Year BBB
Loan at the End of Year 1

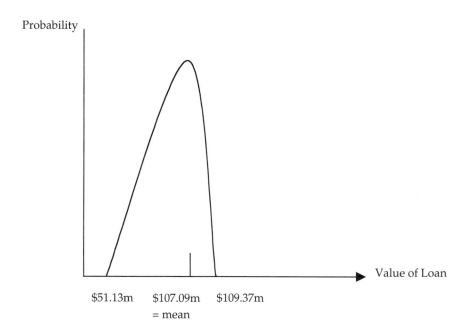

a bad year, how much can it expect to lose with a certain probability? We could define a "bad year" as occurring once every 20
years (the 5 percent VAR) or once every 100 years (the 1 percent
VAR). This definition is similar to market risk VAR except that,
for credit risk, the risk horizon is 1 year rather than 1 day.

Assuming that loan values are normally distributed, the
variance of loan value (in millions) around its mean is $8.9477
(squared), and its standard deviation, or volatility, is the square
root of the variance equal to $2.99. Thus, the 5 percent VAR for the
loan is $1.65 \times \$2.99 = \$4.93$ million. The 1 percent VAR is $2.33 \times
\$2.99 = \$6.97$ million. However, this likely underestimates the ac-
tual or true VAR of the loan because, as shown in Figure 4.2, the
distribution of the loan's value is clearly not normal. In particular,
it demonstrates a negative skew or a long-tailed downside risk.

Table 4.3   VAR Calculations for the BBB Loan (Benchmark Is Mean Value of Loan)

Year-End Rating	Probability of State (%)	New Loan Value Plus Coupon (millions)	Probability Weighted Value ($)	Difference of Value from Mean ($)	Probability Weighted Difference Squared
AAA	0.02	$109.37	0.02	2.28	0.0010
AA	0.33	109.19	0.36	2.10	0.0146
A	5.95	108.66	6.47	1.57	0.1474
BBB	86.93	107.55	93.49	0.46	0.1853
BB	5.30	102.02	5.41	(5.06)	1.3592
B	1.17	98.10	1.15	(8.99)	0.9446
CCC	0.12	83.64	1.10	(23.45)	0.6598
Default	0.18	51.13	0.09	(55.96)	5.6358
			$107.09 = mean value		8.9477 = variance of value

σ = Standard deviation = $2.99

Assuming normal distribution
$\left.\begin{array}{l}\end{array}\right\}$
5 percent VAR = 1.65 × σ = $4.93.
1 percent VAR = 2.33 × σ = $6.97.

Assuming actual distribution*
$\left.\begin{array}{l}\end{array}\right\}$
5 percent VAR = $\dfrac{95 \text{ percent of}}{\text{Actual distribution}}$ = $107.09 − $102.02 = $5.07.

1 percent VAR = $\dfrac{99 \text{ percent of}}{\text{Actual distribution}}$ = $107.09 − $98.10 = $8.99.

*Note: 5% VAR approximated by 6.77% VAR (i.e., 5.3% + 1.17% + 0.12% + 0.18%) and 1% VAR approximated by 1.47% VAR (i.e., 1.17% + 0.12% + 0.18%).
Source: CREDITMETRICS-Technical Document, April 2, 1997, p. 28.

Using the actual distribution of loan values and probabilities in Table 4.3, we can see that there is a 6.77 percent probability that the loan value will fall below $102.02, implying an "approximate" 5 percent actual VAR ($107.09 − $102.02 = $5.07 million), and there is a 1.47 percent probability that the loan value will fall below $98.10, implying an "approximate" 1 percent actual VAR ($107.09 − $98.10 = $8.99). These actual VARs could be made less approximate by using linear interpolation to get at the 5 percent and 1 percent VAR measures. For example, because the 1.47 percentile equals $98.10 and the 0.3 percentile equals $83.64, using linear interpolation, the 1.00 percentile equals approximately $92.29. This suggests an actual 1 percent VAR of $107.09 − $92.29 = $14.80.[11]

Capital Requirements

It is interesting to compare these VAR figures with the 8 percent risk-based capital requirement against loans, currently mandated by the Federal Reserve and the BIS. For a $100 million face (book) value BBB loan to a private-sector borrower, the capital requirement would be $8 million. (Note the contrast to the two VAR measures developed above.) Using the 1 percent VAR based on the normal distribution, the capital requirement against unexpected losses on the loan would be $6.97 million (i.e., less than the BIS requirement). Using the 1 percent VAR based on the interpolated value from the actual distribution, the capital requirement would be $14.80 million (an amount much greater than the BIS capital requirement).[12] Using the CreditMetrics approach, every loan is likely to have a different VAR and thus a different implied or economic capital requirement. This contrasts with the current BIS regulations, in which all loans of different ratings (AAA to CCC) and different maturities are subject to the same 8 percent capital requirement. Moreover, the question of a stress-test multiplier for

---

[11] In the calculation in Table 4.3, we looked at the risk of the loan from the perspective of its mean or expected forward value ($107.09). Using an alternative perspective, we would look at the distribution of changes in value around the value of the loan if it continued to be rated BBB over the whole loan period. In Table 4.2, the forward value of the loan, if its rating remains unchanged over its remaining life, is $107.55. Using this BBB benchmark value, the mean and the variance of the value changes are, respectively, mean = −$0.46 and σ = $3.13. The 1 percent VAR under the normal distribution assumption is then $(2.33 \times -\$3.13) + (-\$0.46) = -\$7.75$.

[12] In 99 years out of 100, the 1 percent VAR capital requirement would allow the bank to survive unexpected credit losses on loans. Note that under the specific risk component for market risk, which measures spread risk, downgrade risk, and concentration risk for tradable instruments like corporate bonds, the 1 percent VAR has to be multiplied by a factor between 3 and 4, and the sensitivity period is 10 days rather than one year.

an internally based capital requirement would also need to be addressed. In particular, the 99 percent loss-of-value estimate can be expected to have a distribution as well. In extremely bad (catastrophic) years, the loss will exceed, by a significant margin, the 99 percent measure calculated here. Under the BIS approach to market risk, this extreme loss or stress-test issue is addressed by requiring banks to multiply their VAR number by a factor ranging between 3 and 4. Research by Boudoukh, Richardson, and Whitelaw (1995) has shown (in simulation exercises) that, for some financial assets, the 3-to-4 multiplication factor may well pick up extreme losses such as the mean in the tail beyond the 99th percentile.[13] Applying such a multiplication factor to low-quality loans would raise capital requirements considerably. The appropriate size of such a multiplication factor, given the problems of stress-testing credit risk models (see Chapter 11), remains a moot point.

TECHNICAL ISSUES AND PROBLEMS

In this section, we will address some of the main technical issues surrounding CreditMetrics. Some of these issues (and assumptions) can be incorporated quite smoothly into the basic model; others are less easy to deal with.

Rating Migration

A number of issues arise when we use the bond-rating transitions assumed in Table 4.1 to calculate the probabilities of moving to different rating categories (or to default) over the one-year horizon.

First, underlying the calculation of the transition numbers, which involves averaging one-year transitions over a past data

---

[13] However, they also found that the 3-to-4 multiplication factor badly underestimated extreme losses if there are "runs" of bad periods (e.g., as might be expected in a major long-term economic contraction).

period (e.g., 20 years), is an important assumption about the way defaults and transitions occur.[14] Specifically, we assume that the transition probabilities follow a stable Markov process [see Altman and Kao (1992)], which means that the probability that a bond or loan will move to any particular state during this period is independent of (not correlated with) any outcome in the past period. However, there is evidence that rating transitions are autocorrelated over time. For example, a bond or loan that was downgraded in the previous period has a higher probability (compared to a loan that was not downgraded) of being downgraded in the current period [see, for example, the results in Nickell, Perraudin, and Varotto (1998)]. This suggests that a second or higher Markov process may better describe rating transitions over time.

The second issue involves transition matrix stability. The use of a single transition matrix assumes that transitions do not differ across borrower types (e.g., industrial firms versus banks, or the United States versus Japan) or across time (e.g., peaks versus troughs in the business cycle). Indeed, there is considerable evidence to suggest that important industry factors, country factors, and business cycle factors impact rating transitions [see Nickell et al. (1998)]. For example, when we examine a loan to a Japanese industrial company, we may need to use a rating transition matrix built around data for that country and industry. Indeed, Credit-PortfolioView, discussed in Chapter 5, can be viewed as a direct attempt to deal with the issue of cyclical impact on the bond/loan transition matrix.[15]

---

[14] Using the simple approach to calculating a transition matrix, suppose we have data for 1997 and 1998. In 1997, 5.0 percent of bonds rated BBB were downgraded to B. In 1998, 5.6 percent of bonds rated BBB were downgraded to B. The average transition probability of being downgraded from BBB to B is therefore 5.3 percent.

[15] Currently, CreditMetrics is developing modifications to its software to allow for cyclicality to be incorporated in the transition matrix.

The third issue relates to the portfolio of bonds used in calculating the transition matrix. Altman and Kishore (1997) found a noticeable impact of bond "aging" on the probabilities calculated in the transition matrix. Indeed, a material difference is noted, depending on whether the bond sample used to calculate transitions is based on new bonds or on all bonds outstanding in a rating class at a particular moment in time.

The fourth issue relates to using bond transition matrices to value loans. As noted earlier, to the extent that collateral, covenants, and other features make loans behave differently from bonds, using bond transition matrices may result in an inherent valuation bias. This suggests that the internal development, by banks, of loan rating transitions (e.g., on a 1–10 scale) based on historic loan databases, might be viewed as crucial in improving the accuracy of VAR measures of loan risk.[16]

Valuation

In the VAR calculation shown earlier in this chapter, the amount recoverable on default (assumed to be $51.13 per $100), the forward zero interest rates (r_i), and the credit spreads (s_i) are all nonstochastic. Making any or all of them stochastic generally will increase any VAR calculation and capital requirement. In particular, loan recovery rates have quite substantial variability [see Carty and Lieberman (1996)], and the credit spread on, say, an AA loan might be expected to vary over some rating class at any moment in time (e.g., AA+ and AA− bonds or loans are likely to have different credit spreads). More generally, credit spreads and interest rates are likely to vary over time, with the credit-cycle, and shifts in the term structure, rather than being deterministic.

---

[16] An alternative would be to use KMV's rating transition matrix, which is built around KMV's EDF scores. The correlation between KMV's transitions and rating agencies' transitions is low.

Regarding recovery rates, if the standard deviation of recovery rates is $25.45 around a mean value of $51.13 per $100 of loans, it can be shown that the 99 percent VAR for the loan under the normal distribution will increase to 2.33 × $3.18 million = $7.38 million, or a VAR-based capital requirement of 7.38 percent of the face value of the BBB loan.[17] One reason for assuming that interest rates are nonstochastic or deterministic is to separate market risk from credit risk,[18] but this remains highly controversial, especially to those who feel that their measurement should be integrated rather than separated and that credit risk is positively correlated with the interest rate cycle. [See also Crouhy and Mark (1998).]

Mark-to-Market Model versus Default Model

By allowing for the effects of credit rating changes (and hence, spread changes) on loan values, as well as default, CreditMetrics can be viewed as a mark-to-market (MTM) model. Other models—for example, CreditRisk plus—view spread risk as part of market risk and concentrate on expected and unexpected loss calculations rather than on expected and unexpected changes in value (or VAR) as in CreditMetrics. This alternative approach is often called the default model or default mode (DM).

It is useful to compare the effects of the MTM model versus the DM model by calculating the expected and, more importantly, the unexpected losses for the same example (the BBB loan) considered above.

Table 4.1 shows that, in a two-state, default–no-default world, the probability of default is $p = 0.18$ percent and the probability of no default $(1 - p)$ is 99.82 percent. After default, the recovery rate is $51.13 per $100 (see Table 4.2), and the loss given default (LGD)

---

[17] CreditMetrics, Technical Document, p. 30; see note 2.

[18] The assumption of nonstochastic interest rates is also consistent with Merton (1974). Nevertheless, Shimko, Tejima, and van Deventer (1993) have extended the Merton model to include stochastic interest rates.

is 1 minus the recovery rate, or $48.87 per $100. The book value exposure amount of the BBB loan is $100 million.

Given these figures, the expected loss on the loan is:

$$\text{Expected loss} = p \times \text{LGD} \times \text{Exposure}$$
$$= .0018 \times .4887 \times \$100,000,000 \qquad (4.3)$$
$$= \$87,966$$

To calculate the unexpected loss, we have to make some assumptions regarding the distribution of default probabilities and recoveries. The simplest assumption is that recoveries are fixed and are independent of the distribution of probabilities (see Chapter 9 for more discussion). Moreover, because the borrower either defaults or does not default, the probability of default can (most simply) be assumed to be binomially distributed with a standard deviation of:

$$\sigma = \sqrt{p(1-p)} \qquad (4.4)$$

Given a fixed recovery rate and exposure amount, the unexpected loss on the loan is:

$$\text{Unexpected loss} = \sqrt{p(1-p)} \times \text{LGD} \times \text{Exposure}$$
$$= \sqrt{(.0018)(.9982)} \times .4887 \times \$100,000,000 \qquad (4.5)$$
$$= \$2,071,511$$

To make this number comparable with the VAR number calculated under CreditMetrics for the normal distribution, we can see that the one standard deviation loss of value (VAR) on the loan is $2.99 million versus $2.07 million under the DM approach.[19] This

---

[19] Or, using the "99th percentile" comparison: 2.33 × $2.99 = $6.97 million versus 2.33 × $2.07 = $4.82 million.

difference occurs partly because the MTM approach allows an upside as well as a downside to the loan's value, and the DM approach fixes the maximum upside value of the loan to its book or face value of $100 million. Thus, economic capital under the DM approach is more closely related to book value accounting concepts than to the market value accounting concepts used in the MTM approach.

SUMMARY

In this chapter, we have outlined the VAR approach to calculating the capital requirement on a loan or a bond. We have used one nonproprietary application of the VAR methodology—CreditMetrics—to illustrate the approach and raise the technical issues involved. Its key characteristics are: (1) it involves a full valuation or MTM approach in which both an upside and a downside to loan values are considered, and (2) the analyst can consider the actual distribution of estimated future loan values in calculating a capital requirement on a loan. We will revisit VAR methodology and CreditMetrics again in Chapter 10, when we consider calculating the VAR and capital requirements for a loan portfolio.

Appendix **4.1**

Calculating the Forward Zero Curve for Loan Valuation

1. *The Current Yield Curve (CYC)*

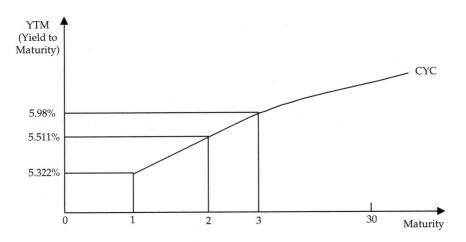

From the current yield curve (CYC) for coupon bonds, shown above, a zero yield curve (ZYC) for zero-coupon bonds can be derived using "no arbitrage" pricing relationships between coupon bonds and zero coupon bonds, and solving by successive substitution.

2. *Calculation of the Current Zero Curve Using No Arbitrage*

One-year zero: $100 = \dfrac{C+F}{(1+Y_1)} = \dfrac{C+F}{(1+Z_1)} = \dfrac{105.322}{(1.05322)}$

$$\therefore Z_1 = 5.322 \text{ percent}$$

Two-year zero: $100 = \dfrac{C}{(1+Y_2)} + \dfrac{F+C}{(1+Y_2)^2} = \dfrac{C}{(1+Z_1)} + \dfrac{F+C}{(1+Z_2)^2}$

$$100 = \dfrac{5.511}{(1.05511)} + \dfrac{105.511}{(1.05511)^2} = \dfrac{5.511}{(1.05322)} + \dfrac{105.511}{(1.055162)^2}$$

$$\therefore Z_2 = 5.5162 \text{ percent}$$

3. *Comparison of the Zero Yield Curve (ZYC) and Current Yield Curve (CYC)*

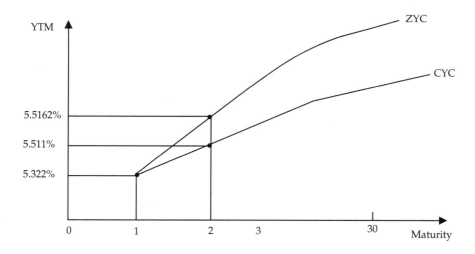

The next step is to derive the one-year forward rates implied by the current zero yield curve $(f_1, f_2, \dots, f_n)$.

4. *Derivation of the One-Year Forward Rates Using Current Zero Rates*

$$1+f_1 = \frac{(1+Z_2)^2}{(1+Z_1)}$$

$$1+f_1 = \frac{(1.055162)^2}{(1.05322)} = 1.0571 \therefore f_1 = 5.71 \text{ percent}$$

$$1+f_2 = \frac{(1+Z_3)^3}{(1+Z_2)^2} \text{ etc.}$$

We can then use the expectations theory of the yield curve to derive the ZYC expected next year, or the forward zero curve $(Z'_1, Z'_2 \ldots)$.

5. *Derivation of One-Year Forward Government Yield Curve* (Z'_i) *Using Expectations Theory*

$$\left(1+Z'_1\right) = 1+f_1$$

$$\left(1+Z'_2\right) = \sqrt{(1+f_1)(1+f_2)}$$

$$\cdot$$
$$\cdot$$
$$\cdot$$

$$\left(1+Z'_{29}\right) = \sqrt[29]{(1+f_1)+\ldots+(1+f_{29})}$$

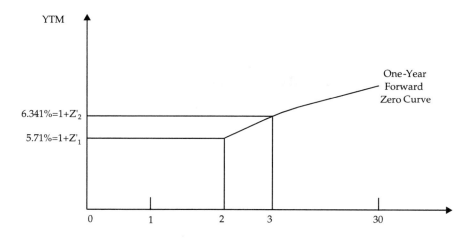

For valuation, fixed credit spreads (s_i) for each maturity are added to the forward zero curve.

Chapter **5**

The Macro Simulation Approach: The McKinsey Model and Other Models

INTRODUCTION

As discussed in Chapter 4, the current methodology underlying CreditMetrics VAR calculations assumes that transition probabilities are stable across borrower types and across the business cycle. The assumption of stability is important. A recent survey of the internal rating systems of 18 major bank holding companies suggested that as much as 60 percent of their collective loan portfolios may be below the equivalent of investment grade [Treacy and Carey (1998)], and the default rates on low-quality credits (including junk bonds) are highly sensitive to the state of the business cycle. Moreover, there is empirical evidence that rating transitions in general may depend on the state of the economy [see Nickell, Perraudin, and Varotto (1998) and Wilson (1997a, 1997b)]. This evidence suggests that the probability of downgrades and defaults may be significantly greater in a cyclical downturn than in an upturn.

DEALING WITH CYCLICAL FACTORS

There are at least two ways to deal with cyclical factors and effects:

1. Divide the past sample period into recession years and nonrecession years, and calculate two separate historic transition matrices (a recession matrix and a nonrecession matrix) to yield two separate VAR calculations.

2. Directly model the relationship between transition probabilities and macro factors, and, when a model is fitted, simulate the evolution of transition probabilities over time by generating macro-"shocks" to the model.

The second approach is taken by McKinsey's CreditPortfolioView. In this chapter, we illustrate the basic dynamics of a model similar to that of Wilson (1997a and 1997b), but within a single-country context.

THE MACRO SIMULATION APPROACH

The essential idea is represented in the transition matrix for a given country, shown in Figure 5.1. Note especially the cell of the matrix in the bottom right-hand corner (p_{CD}).

Each cell in the transition matrix shows the probability that a particular counterparty, rated at a given grade at the beginning of the period, will move to another rating by the end of the period. In Figure 5.1, p_{CD} shows the estimated probability that a C-rated borrower (a speculative-grade borrower) will default over the next year—that is, it will move from a C rating to a D (default) rating.

In general, one would expect this probability to move significantly during the business cycle and to be higher in recessions than in expansions. Because the probabilities in each row of the transition matrix must sum to 1, an increase in p_{CD} must be compensated for by a decrease in other probabilities—for example, those involving upgrades of initially C-rated debt, where p_{CB} and p_{CA} represent the probabilities of the C-rated borrower's moving to, respectively, a B grade and an A grade during the next year. The

Figure 5.1   Historic (Unconditional) Transition Matrix

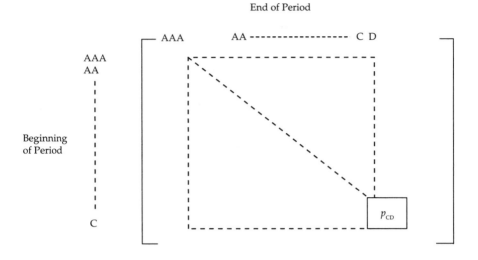

density, or mass, of the probabilities in the transition matrix moves increasingly in a southeast direction as a recession proceeds.[1]

With this in mind, let p_{CD} vary at time t along with a set of macro factors indexed by variable y. For convenience, the subscripts (C and D) will be dropped. However, we are implicitly modeling the probability that a C-rated borrower will default over the next period (say, 1 year). In general terms:[2]

$$p_t = f(y_t) \tag{5.1}$$

where $f' < 0$; that is, there is an inverse link between the state of the economy and the probability of default. The macro indicator variable y_t can be viewed as being driven by a set of i (systematic)

---

[1] In fact, all the probabilities in the final column of the transition matrix (p_{AAAD}, p_{AAD}, and so on) will move cyclically and can be modeled in a fashion similar to p_{CD}.

[2] In Wilson (1997a and 1997b), equation (5.1) is modeled as a logistic function of the form $p_t = 1/(1 + e^{-y_t})$. This constrains p to lie between 0 and 1.

macro economic variables at time t (X_{it}) as well as (unsystematic) random shocks or innovations to the economic system (V_t). In general:

$$y_t = g(X_{it}, V_t) \tag{5.2}$$

where $i = 1, \ldots, n$ and $V_t \sim N(0, \sigma)$

In turn, macro economic variables (X_{it}) such as gross domestic product (GDP) growth, unemployment, and so on, can themselves be viewed as being determined by their past histories (e.g., lagged GDP growth) as well as being sensitive to shocks themselves (ε_{it}).[3] Thus:

$$X_{it} = h(X_{it-1}, X_{it-2}, \ldots \varepsilon_{it}) \tag{5.3}$$

Different macro model specifications can be used in the context of equations (5.2) and (5.3) to improve model fit, and different models can be used to explain transitions for different countries and industries.

Substituting equation (5.3) into equation (5.2), and equation (5.2) into equation (5.1), the probability of a speculative (grade C) loan moving to grade D during the next year will be determined by:

$$p_t = f(X_{it-j}; V_t, \varepsilon_{it}) \tag{5.4}$$

Essentially, equation (5.4) models the determinants of this transition probability as a function of lagged macro variables, a general economic shock factor or "innovation" (V_t), and shock factors or innovations for each of the i macro variables (ε_{it}). Because the X_{it-j} are predetermined, the key variables driving p_t will be the

---

[3] In Wilson (1997a), the macro variables are modeled as levels of variables (rather than changes in levels), and the X_{it} variables are related to their lagged values by a second-order autoregressive process.

innovations or shocks V_t and ε_{it}. Using a structured Monte Carlo simulation approach, values for V_t and ε_{it} can be generated for periods in the future that occur with the same probability as that observed from history.[4] We can use the simulated V's and ε's, along with the fitted macro model, to simulate scenario values for p_{CD} in periods $t, t+1, t+2, \ldots, t+n$, and on into the future.

Suppose that, based on current macro conditions, the simulated value for p_{CD}, labeled p^*, is .35, and the number in the historic (unconditional) transition matrix is .3 (where * indicates the simulated value of the transition probability). Because the (unconditional) transition value of .3 is less than the value estimated conditional on the macro economic state (.35), we are likely to underestimate the VAR of loans and a loan portfolio—especially at the low-quality end.

Define the ratio (r_t):

$$r_t = \frac{p^*_t}{p_t} = \frac{.35}{.3} = 1.16 \tag{5.5}$$

Based on the simulated macro model, the probability of a C-rated borrower's defaulting over the next year is 16 percent higher than the average (unconditional) historical transition relationship implies. We can also calculate this ratio for periods $t+1, t+2$, and so on. For example, suppose, based on simulated innovations and macro-factor relationships, the simulation predicts p^*_{t+1} to be .38. The ratio relevant for the next year (r_{t+1}) is then:

$$r_{t+1} = \frac{p^*_{t+1}}{p_{t+1}} = \frac{.38}{.3} = 1.267 \tag{5.6}$$

---

[4] Technically, the variances and covariances of V_t and ε_{it} are calculated from the fitted model (the Σ matrix). The Σ matrix is then decomposed using the Cholesky decomposition $\Sigma = AA'$, where A and A' are symmetric matrices and A' is the transpose of A. Shocks can be simulated by multiplying the matrix A' by a random number generator: $Z_t \sim N(0,1)$.

Again, the unconditional transition matrix will underestimate the risk of default on low-grade loans in this period.

These calculated ratios can be used to adjust the elements in the projected $t, t+1, \ldots, t+n$ transition matrices. In McKinsey's CreditPortfolioView, the unconditional value of p_{CD} is adjusted by the ratio of the conditional value of p_{CD} to its unconditional value. Consider the transition matrix for period t; then $r_t \times .3 = .35$ (which is the same as p^*t). Thus, we replace .3 with .35 in the transition matrix (M_t), as shown in Figure 5.2. This also means that we need to adjust all the other elements in the transition matrix (e.g., p_{CA}, p_{CB}, and so on). A number of procedures can be used to do this, including linear and nonlinear regressions of each element or cell in the transition matrix on the ratio r_t [see Wilson (1997a and 1997b); remember that the rows of the transition matrix

Figure 5.2   Conditional Transition Matrix M_t

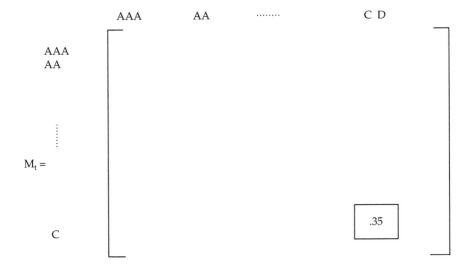

Figure 5.3 Conditional Transition Matrix M_{t+1}

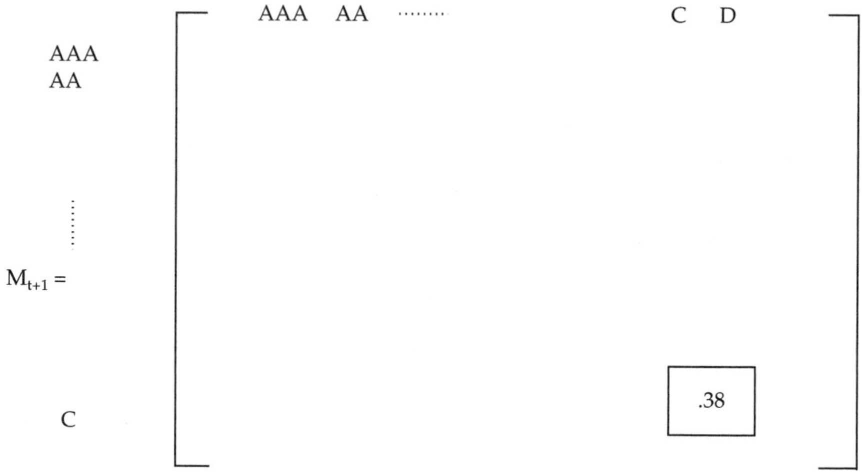

must sum to one[5]]. For the next period $(t+1)$, the transition matrix would have to be similarly adjusted by multiplying the unconditional value of p by r_{t+1}, or $.3 \times 1.267 = .38$. This is shown in Figure 5.3.

Thus, there would be different transition matrices for each year into the future $(t, t+1, \ldots t+n)$, reflecting the simulated effect of the macro economic shocks on transition probabilities. We could use this type of approach, along with CreditMetrics, to calculate a cyclically sensitive VAR for one year, two years, ... n years.[6]

---

[5] The precise procedure for doing this is described in the *Approach Document* to CreditPortfolioView, pp. 80–94. Basically, it involves the use of a shift operator (called the systematic risk sensitivity parameter) along with the imposition of the constraint that the shifted values in each row of the migration matrix sum to one.

[6] Alternatively, using a default model [and a default (p)/no default $(1 - p)$ setup], unexpected loss rates can be calculated for different stages of the business cycle.

Specifically, the simulated transition matrix M_t would replace the historically based unconditional (stable Markov) transition matrix, and, given any current rating for the loan (say, C), the distribution of loan values based on the macro-adjusted transition probabilities in the C row of the matrix M_t could be used to calculate VAR at the one-year horizon, in a fashion similar to that used under CreditMetrics in Chapter 4.

We could also calculate VAR estimates using longer horizons. Suppose we are interested in transitions over the next two years (t and $t + 1$). Multiplying the two matrixes,

$$M_{t't+1} = M_t \times M_{t+1} \tag{5.7}$$

produces a new matrix, $M_{t't+1}$. The final column of this new matrix will give the simulated (cumulative) probabilities of default on differently rated loans over the next two years.

Figure 5.4 Probability Distribution of Simulated Values of p^*_t in Year t

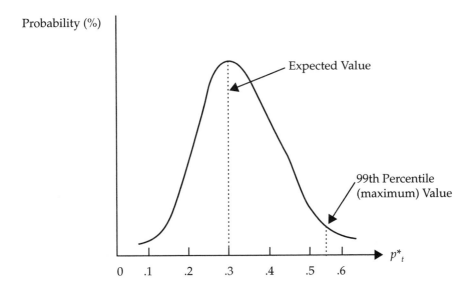

We have considered just one simulation of values for p^*_t from one set of shocks (V_t, ε_{it}). Repeating the exercise over and over again (e.g., taking 10,000 random draws) would produce 10,000 values of p^*_t and 10,000 possible transition matrices.

Consider the current year (t). We can plot hypothetical simulated values for p^*_t as shown in Figure 5.4. The mean simulated value of p^*_t is .3, but the extreme value (99th percentile, or worst-case value) is .55. When calculating capital requirements—that is, when considering unexpected declines in loan values—the latter figure for p^*_t, and the transition matrix associated with this value, might be considered most relevant.

SUMMARY

One way to build in business cycle effects and to take a forward-looking view of VAR is to model macro effects, both systematic and unsystematic, on the probability of default and associated rating transitions. The macro simulation approach should be viewed as being complementary to CreditMetrics, overcoming some of the biases resulting from assuming static or stationary transition probabilities period to period.[7]

---

[7] The unexpected loss rate could also be simulated using this type of model for a "two-state" world of default versus no-default, rather than a full VAR model.

Chapter 6

The Risk-Neutral Valuation Approach: KPMG's Loan Analysis System (LAS) and Other Models

Introduction

The use of risk-neutral (RN) probabilities to value risky assets has been in the finance literature at least as far back as Arrow (1953) and has been subsequently developed by Harrison and Kreps (1979), Harrison and Pliska (1981), and Kreps (1982). In finance, it has been traditional to value risky assets by discounting cash flows on an asset by a risk-adjusted discount rate. To do this, one needs to know a probability distribution for cash flows and the risk–return preferences of investors. The latter are especially difficult to deal with. Suppose, however, it is assumed that assets trade in a market where *all* investors are willing to accept, from any risky asset, the same expected return as that promised by the risk-free asset. Such a market can be described as behaving in a "risk-neutral" fashion. In a financial market where investors behave in a risk-neutral fashion, the prices of all assets can be determined by simply discounting the expected future cash flows on the asset by the risk-free rate.[1]

---

[1] For pricing of derivative assets, when the underlying asset is traded, the risk-neutral price is the correct one, irrespective of investor preferences. This is because, with an underlying asset, the derivative can be perfectly hedged to create a riskless portfolio. When a portfolio is riskless, it has an expected return equal to the risk-free rate.

The equilibrium relationship—where the expected return on a risky asset equals the risk-free rate—can be utilized to back-out an implied RN probability of default (also called the equivalent martingale measure). This forward-looking estimate of the default risk of a security can be compared with historical measures of transition probabilities (often called "natural" measures). As long as an asset is risky, the forward-looking RN probability will not equal its natural measure (the realized value of the transition probability).[2]

In this chapter, we discuss two ways of deriving forward-looking default probability measures based on the RN valuation approach. We then look at the relationship between the RN measure of default and its historical (natural) measure. Finally, we look at the potential use of the RN concept in pricing loans and in calculating the market value of a loan (and, potentially, its VAR).

DERIVING RN PROBABILITIES

This section explains, as simply as possible, two approaches to deriving RN probability measures.

Deriving RN Measures from Spreads on Zero-Coupon Bonds

One approach to deriving RN probabilities from spreads between risky bonds (e.g., corporate bonds) and Treasuries has been used at Goldman Sachs and was described by Litterman and Iben (1989).

Consider the two zero-coupon bond yield curves shown in Figure 6.1. The (annualized) discount yield on one-year zero Treasuries is 10 percent, and the (annualized) discount yield on one-year grade B zero corporates is 15.8 percent. The methodology assumes that zero yield curves either exist or can be fitted. As

---

[2] For an excellent discussion of the theory underlying RN probabilities, see Sundaram (1997).

Figure 6.1 The Zero-Coupon Treasury Bond Curve and the Zero-Coupon Corporate Grade B Curve

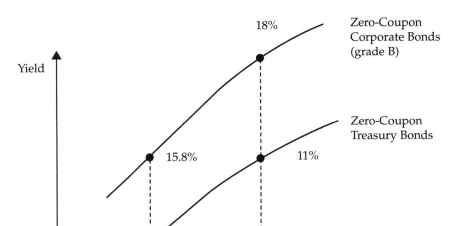

noted above, in equilibrium, under RN valuation, the expected return on the risky bond must equal the risk-free return (the return on the risk-free Treasury bond) or:

$$p_1 (1 + k_1) = 1 + i_1 \qquad (6.1)$$

where p_1 = the implied RN probability of repayment in year 1,
$1 + k_1$ = the promised return on the (risky) one-year corporate bond,
$1 + i_1$ = the risk-free return on the one-year Treasury bond.

For simplicity, we assume that if the risky bond defaults, the loss given default (LGD) = 1 and the bondholder receives nothing.

From equation (6.1), we can back-out the implied RN probability of repayment (p_1):[3]

$$p_1 = \frac{1+i_1}{1+k_1} = \frac{1.1}{1.158} = .95 \tag{6.2}$$

Thus, the RN probability of default p^*_1 is:

$$p^*_1 = 1 - p_1 = 1 - .95 = .05 \tag{6.3}$$

We can also derive the RN probability of default in year 2 . . . year n by exploiting forward rates impounded in the zero curves in Figure 6.1. For example, p^*_2, the RN probability of default in year 2 (essentially, the forward marginal probability that the grade B corporate borrower will default between year 1 and year 2), can be derived in a two-step process. The first step is to derive the one-year expected forward rates on corporates and Treasuries from the existing zero curves. The second step is to back-out the implied RN probability of default from the forward rates. (See Appendix 6.1.) By utilizing this approach, a whole term structure of forward-looking RN probabilities can be derived.

Deriving the RN Probability Measure from Stock Prices

Using bond prices and yield spreads, the preceding approach extracted the RN probability of default forecast for a particular borrower. This involved placing the borrower into a particular rating class (and, thus, a matched yield curve for that rating class) and utilized relationships between zero-coupon bond prices and yields for risky versus risk-free debt. An alternative approach, described by Delianedis and Geske (1998), is to exploit the type of option pricing models discussed in Chapter 3, along with stock prices

---

[3] Alternatively, the probability of default can be shown in terms of bond prices:

$$\text{of default} = 1 - \frac{\text{Price of 1-year corporate zero}}{\text{Price of 1-year government zero}} = 1 - \frac{\$86.356}{\$90.909} = .05$$

and the volatility of stock prices. An RN probability forecast for a particular borrower can also be backed-out of an option-pricing model (OPM). Indeed, from a Merton-type model, where equity is viewed as a call option on the value of the firm's assets, the probability that the value of a firm's assets at the time of debt maturity (e.g., $T = 1$) will be greater than the face value of the firm's debt is $N_1(k)$. The RN probability of default is then:

$$p^*_1 = 1 - (N_1(k)) \qquad (6.4)$$

As shown in Appendix 6.2, $N_1(k)$ is the area under the normal distribution relating to a variable k, which, in turn, depends on the value of the firm's assets, the volatility of the firm's assets, leverage, time to maturity, and the risk-free rate. Similar to the KMV approach, neither the market value nor the volatility of the firm's assets is directly observable. These values have to be iterated from observable stock prices and the volatility of stock prices. Delianedis and Geske (1998), using (1) the RN probabilities derived from a standard Merton (1974) model, and (2) the RN probabilities derived from a richer Merton-type model [based on Geske (1977)] that allows for multiple classes of debt, show the ability of these measures to forecast actual rating transitions and defaults. In other words, the RN measure has the potential to predict changes in the natural measure.[4]

THE RELATIONSHIP BETWEEN THE RN MEASURE AND THE NATURAL MEASURE OF DEFAULT PROBABILITY

This relationship has been explored by Ginzberg, Maloney, and Wilner (1994), Belkin et al. of KPMG (1998a–d), and Crouhy and Mark (1998), among others.

Following Ginzberg et al. (1994) and Belkin et al. (1998a–d), the relationship between the RN measure and the natural measure of

---

[4] The Merton (1974) model assumes all long-term debt is of equal seniority and is unsecured.

default probability can be best viewed in terms of a risk premium. That is, the spread (ϕ) between the returns on a one-year risk-free and risky asset (such as a corporate bond) will reflect the RN probability of default (p^*_1) and some loss given default (LGD):

$$\phi_1 = p^*_1 \times \text{LGD} \tag{6.5}$$

Alternatively, we can think of the spread as compensating investors for both an expected loss (ε_1) and an unexpected loss (u_1) on the risky bond:

$$\phi_1 = \varepsilon_1 + u_1 \tag{6.6}$$

The expected loss (ε_1) can, in turn, be set equal to the average or natural probability of default of this type of borrower by multiplying the historic transition probability (t_1) times the LGD:[5]

$$\varepsilon_1 = t_1 \times \text{LGD} \tag{6.7}$$

The unexpected loss component (u_1) can be viewed as being equal to the unexpected probability of default times the LGD.[6]

Substituting equation (6.7) into equation (6.6) and incorporating equation (6.5), we have:

$$p^*_1 \times \text{LGD} = (t_1 \times \text{LGD}) + u_1 \tag{6.8}$$

Thus, given some fixed LGD, the difference between p^*_1 (the RN probability of default) and t_1 (the natural probability of default) is a risk premium that reflects the unexpected default probability.

For example, if $\phi_1 = 1$ percent, LGD $= 40$ percent, and $t_1 = 1$ percent, then:

---

[5] For example, the historic probability of a grade B borrower entering into default during the next year.

[6] Unlike CreditMetrics, where the VAR (or unexpected loss in value) is loan-specific, these unexpected losses are rating-class-specific. Moreover, CreditMetrics allows for upgrade and downgrade effects on loan value whereas the simple RN model assumes either default or no default.

$$\phi_1 = p^*_1 \times \text{LGD} = (t_1 \times \text{LGD}) + u_1$$
$$\phi_1 = p^*_1 \times .4 = (.01 \times .4) + u_1 = .01 \tag{6.9}$$

We can then solve for values of both p^*_1 (the RN probability) and u_1 (the unexpected loss premium).

From equation (6.9), the RN probability of default $p^*_1 = 2.5$ percent [which is higher than the natural (historic) default probability of $t_1 = 1$ percent] and the unexpected loss or risk premium is 0.6 percent.

Ginzberg et al. (1994) offer some calculations to show how actual U.S. credit spreads can be broken down into an expected loss and a risk premium component. For example, an average (par) spread of 20.01 basis points on one-year AAA corporates over one-year Treasuries can be broken down into an expected loss component $(t_1 \times \text{LGD})$ of 0.01 basis points and a risk premium (u_1) of 20 basis points. An 1188.97 basis-point spread on one-year CCC bonds over Treasuries can be broken down into an expected loss component of 918.97 basis points and an unexpected loss component of 270 basis points.

RISK-NEUTRAL PROBABILITIES AND VALUATION

Risk-neutral (RN) probabilities have considerable potential value for a banker who must reach pricing decisions and make "market" valuations of loans. For example, RN probabilities can be used in setting the required spread or risk premium on a loan. Following Ginzberg et al. (1994), suppose a banker wants to find the fixed spread *(s)* on a one-year loan that will yield $1 of expected NPV from each $1 lent. (The loan would be a break-even "project" in an NPV sense.) The banker knows that:

r = one-year risk-free rate = 4 percent;

p^*_1 = RN probability of default = 6.5 percent;

LGD = 33.434 percent.

To solve for s:

$$E(\text{NPV}) = \frac{\left[(1-p^*_1)(1+r+s)\right] + p^*_1(1-LGD)}{1+r} = 1$$

$$= \frac{\left[(.935)(1.04+s)\right] + .065(.66566)}{1.04}$$

(6.10)

The value of s—the loan spread—that solves equation (6.10) is 2.602 percent.

However, there is a major problem in extending this type of analysis beyond the one-year horizon. The default or no-default scenario, under which RN probabilities are derived, fits the one-year loan case but not the multiyear loan case. For multiyear loans, a richer set of possibilities exist. These include borrower migration upgrades and downgrades, that may trigger some loan repricing "grid" which may in turn affect the value of the loan and the borrower's option to prepay a loan early.

Ginzberg et al. (1994) and KPMG's Loan Analysis System (LAS; 1998) have attempted to extend the valuation framework in equation (6.10) to multiperiod loans with a variety of options— for example, loan spread repricing (as nondefault transitions in credit quality occur)—and to build in penalty fees for borrowers who prepay early.

Figure 6.2, from KPMG (1996), shows, in a simplified fashion, the potential transitions of the credit rating of a B-rated borrower over a four-year loan period. People familiar with bond valuation models, especially lattice or "tree" diagrams for bond valuation, will immediately recognize the similarity. Given transition probabilities, the original grade B borrower can migrate up or down over the loan's life to different nodes (ratings), and may even migrate to D or default (an absorbing state). Along with these migrations, one can build in a pricing grid that reflects the bank's current policy on spread repricing for borrowers of different quality (or, alternatively, a grid that reflects what the "market" charges). Potentially at least, this methodology can tell the bank whether it has a "good" or "bad" repricing grid in an expected net

Figure 6.2 Multiperiod Loan Migrates over Many Periods

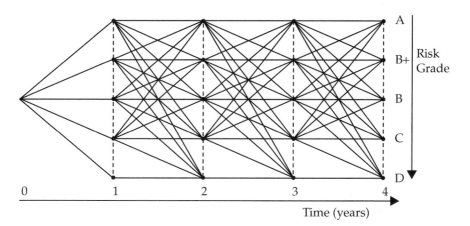

Source: S.D. Aguais, L. Forest, S. Krishnamoorthy, and T. Mueller, "Incorporating New Fixed Income Approaches into Commercial Loan Valuation," *Journal of Lending and Credit Risk Management*, February 1996, pp. 50–65.

present value (NPV) sense (basically, whether $E(\text{NPV}) \gtrless 1$). When valuing a loan in this framework, valuation takes place recursively (from right to left in Figure 6.2), as it does when valuing bonds under binomial or multinomial models. For example, if the $E(\text{NPV})$ of the loan in its final year is too "high," and given some prepayment fee, the model can allow prepayment of the loan to take place at the end of period 3. Working backward through the tree from right to left, the total $E(\text{NPV})$ of the four-year loan can be determined. Moreover, the analyst can make different assumptions about spreads (the pricing grid) at different ratings and prepayment fees to determine the loan's value. Reportedly, other aspects of a loan's structure, such as caps, amortization schedules, and so on, can be built in and a VAR can also be calculated.[7] Appendix 6.3

---

[7] As Belkin, Suchower, and Forest (1998c) have shown, the LAS model can also be used to calculate VAR figures. For example, a simple VAR figure could be calculated by using LAS to value the loan at the one-year (credit-event) horizon. Alternatively, model spread volatility can be introduced by allowing the transitions themselves to be variable (KPMG call this "Z"-risk).

provides a simple example of a loan valuation using a simplified default mode (DM) framework. Following Ginzberg et al. (1994), it can be argued that this extended RN valuation framework is valid as long as a replicating (no-arbitrage) portfolio of underlying assets is available. However, it is unclear how such a replicating portfolio could be established in reality when most loans are not traded in active markets.

SUMMARY

The RN valuation framework provides valuable tools for both default prediction and loan valuation. Compared to historic (data-based) transition probabilities, the RN model gives a forward-looking prediction of default. The RN prediction will generally exceed the history-based transition prediction over some horizon because, conceptually, it contains a risk premium reflecting the unexpected probability of default. Moreover, the RN framework considers only two "credit" states: default and no-default.

Recently, KPMG (1998) suggested a valuation framework that is potentially consistent with the RN model under no-arbitrage. Over its life, a loan can migrate to states other than default/no-default. The valuation model is similar in spirit to a multinomial tree model for bond valuation, except that transition probabilities replace interest rate movement probabilities. This model has some flexibility: credit spreads can vary, fees can be charged on prepayments, and other special provisions can be built into the valuation process. A question arises as to the link between the model and the existence of an underlying portfolio of replicating assets. In particular, the exact details of the construction of a replicating no-arbitrage portfolio for a multiperiod nontradable loan are somewhat unclear.

Deriving RN Probabilities for Year 2 . . . Year *N*

Assume that the expectations theory of interest rates holds, so that, for Treasuries:

$$(1 + i_2)^2 = (1 + i_1)(1 + f_1)$$

Given the data in Figure 6.1:

$$1 + f_1 = \frac{(1 + i_2)^2}{(1 + i_1)} = \frac{(1.11)^2}{(1.10)} = 1.12$$

or f_1 = the expected one-year forward rate on Treasuries = 12 percent.

Similarly, for corporate bonds:

$$1 + c_1 = \frac{(1 + k_2)^2}{(1 + k_1)} = \frac{(1.18)^2}{(1.158)} = 1.202$$

or c_1 = the expected one-year forward rate on corporate grade B bonds = 20.2 percent.

In equilibrium, the expected (forward) return on the risky bond should equal the (expected) risk-free return:

$$p_2 (1 + c_1) = (1 + f_1)$$

Thus:

$$p_2 = \frac{1+f_1}{1+c_1} = \frac{1.12}{1.202} = .9318$$

Consequently, the RN probability of default in year 2 is:

$$p^*_2 = 1 - p_2 = .0682$$
$$\text{or } p^*_2 = 6.82 \text{ percent}$$

We can follow the same methodology to derive p^*_3, p^*_4, and so on.

Deriving RN Probabilities from Equity Values

The explicit form of the BSM call option model for valuing a firm's equity is:

$$E = AN_1\left(k + \sigma_A\sqrt{T-t}\right) - Be^{-r(T-t)}N_1(k)$$

where E = the current market value of equity,
A = the current market value of the firm's assets,
$N(\cdot)$ = cumulative normal distribution function,
σ_A = the variance of the firm's assets,
T = maturity date of debt,
t = current time,
B = the face value of debt,
r = the risk-free rate.

$$k = \frac{\ln(A/B) + \left(r - \sigma_A^2/2\right)(T-t)}{\sigma_A\sqrt{T-t}}$$

where $p^*_i = 1 - N_i(k)$

and p^*_i = the risk neutral probability of default.

Valuation of a Loan Using a E(NPV)-Type Approach

Given here is a simplified example of an $E(\text{NPV})$-type approach to loan valuation in a default mode (DM) framework. We assume:

1. A four-year loan, face value $100 million.
2. Fixed-rate (15 percent) coupon on loan.
3. Risk-free rate each period: $r_i = 4$ percent (thus, the credit spread on the loan is 11 percent).
4. LGD = 1 (no recovery in default).
5. Risk-neutral (RN) probability of default per period $p^*_i = .1$ (thus, the RN probability of repayment is .9).

Given these assumptions (shown in Figure 6.3A), the value of the loan in each year is:

$$E(\text{NPV}_4) = \frac{(.9)^4 \times \$115}{(1.04)^4} = \$64.49 \text{ million}$$

$$E(\text{NPV}_3) = \frac{(.9)^3 \times \$15}{(1.04)^3} = \$9.72$$

$$E(\text{NPV}_2) = \frac{(.9)^2 \times \$15}{(1.04)^2} = \$11.23$$

Figure 6.3A Loan Valuation in a Default Mode (DM) Setting

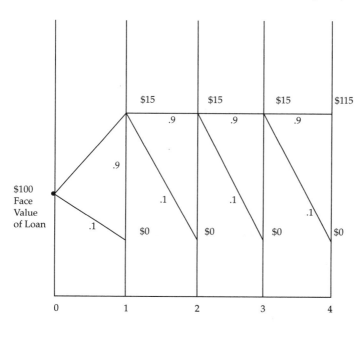

$$E(\text{NPV}_1) = \frac{(.9) \times \$15}{(1.04)} = \$12.98$$

Total $E(\text{NPV}) = \$98.42$ million

This loan is marginally unprofitable from an NPV perspective; the $E(\text{NPV})$ per dollar is $\$.9842$, which is less than $\$1$. This suggests that profitability on this type of loan in the future would be enhanced by either (1) charging upfront fees for loan origination (e.g., an upfront fee of 2 percent of face value, or $\$2$ million) and/or (2) increasing the credit spread (e.g., to 12 percent or a coupon rate of 16 percent per annum). If fees or loan rates are set too high, making the NPV very profitable to the bank, in years 2 and 3, the borrower may seek to prepay the loan early. The bank might then protect itself by imposing an early prepayment penalty on the borrower.

Chapter 7

The Insurance Approach: Mortality Models and the CSFP Credit Risk Plus Model

INTRODUCTION

Surprisingly, only quite recently have ideas from insurance found their way into the new tools for credit risk measurement and management. In this chapter, we look at two applications of insurance ideas—one from life insurance and one from property insurance. Specifically, Altman (1989) and others have developed mortality tables for loans and bonds using ideas (and models) similar to those that insurance actuaries apply when they set premiums for life insurance policies. Crédit Suisse Financial Products (CSFP) has developed a model similar to the one a property insurer selling household fire insurance might use when assessing the risk of policy losses in setting premiums.

We first look at the mortality model and then at the CSFP Credit Risk Plus model.

MORTALITY ANALYSIS

The idea is very simple, based on a portfolio of loans or bonds and their historic default experience, develop a table that can be used in a predictive sense for one-year, or marginal, mortality rates

(MMR) and for multiyear, or cumulative, mortality rates (CMR). Combining such calculations with LGDs can produce estimates of expected losses.[1]

To calculate, say, the MMRs of grade B bonds (loans) defaulting in each year of their "life," the analyst will pick a sample of years—say, 1971 through 1998—and, for *each year*, will look at:

$$\text{MMR}_1 = \frac{\text{Total value of grade B bonds defaulting in year 1 of issue}}{\text{Total value of grade B bonds outstanding in year 1 of issue}} \tag{7.1}$$

$$\text{MMR}_2 = \frac{\text{Total value of grade B bonds defaulting in year 2 of issue}}{\begin{array}{c}\text{Total value of grade B bonds outstanding in year 2}\\ \text{of issue (adjusted for defaults, calls, sinking}\\ \text{fund redemptions, and maturities in the prior year)}\end{array}} \tag{7.2}$$

and so on for $\text{MMR}_3, \ldots, \text{MMR}_n$.

When an individual year MMR_i has been calculated, the analyst calculates a weighted average, which becomes the figure entered into the mortality table. The weights used should reflect the relative issue sizes in different years, thus biasing the results toward the larger-issue years. The average MMR in year 1 for a particular grade $(\overline{\text{MMR}}_1)$ would be calculated as:

$$\overline{\text{MMR}}_1 = \sum_{i=1971}^{1998} \text{MMR}_{1i} \times w_i$$
$$\sum w_i = 1 \tag{7.3}$$

To calculate a cumulative mortality rate (CMR)—the probability that a loan or bond will default over a period longer than a year

---

[1] Combining the volatility of annual MMRs with LGDs can produce unexpected loss calculations as well [see Altman and Saunders (1997)].

(say, 2 years)—it is first necessary to specify the relationship between MMRs and survival rates (SRs):

$$MMR_i = 1 - SR_i$$

or   (7.4)

$$SR_i = 1 - MMR_i$$

Consequently,

$$CMR_N = 1 - \prod_{i=1}^{N} SR_i \qquad (7.5)$$

where Π is the geometric sum or product, $SR_1 \times SR_2 \times \ldots SR_N$, and
N denotes the number of years over which the cumulative mortal-
ity rate is calculated.

Mortality Tables

Table 7.1 shows marginal and cumulative mortality rates for syndicated loans and bonds over a five-year horizon, as computed by
Altman and Suggitt (1997). The table has an interesting feature:
for the higher grades, the mortality rates are quite similar, but
this is not the case for the lowest-quality grades. For example,
low-quality loans have much higher MMR_i in the first three years
of life than similarly rated bonds. The key question is: Is this economically meaningful? In other words, does this result imply
that high-yield loans and bonds have substantially different default characteristics, or could it be a statistical artifact due to a
relatively small sample size? In particular, although not shown,
each of the MMR estimates has an implied standard-error and
confidence interval. Moreover, it can be shown that as the number
of loans or bonds in the sample increases (i.e., as N gets bigger),
the standard error on a mortality rate will fall (i.e., the degree of

Table 7.1 Comparison of Syndicated Bank Loan versus Corporate Bond Mortality Rates, Based on Original Issuance Principal Amounts (1991–1996)

		Years after Issue								
		1 Year		2 Years		3 Years		4 Years		5 Years	
		Bank	Bond	Bank	Bond	Bank	Bond	Bank	Bond	Bank	Bond
AAA	Marginal	0.00%	0.00%	0.00%	0.00%	0.00%	0.00%	0.00%	0.00%	0.00%	0.00%
	Cumulative	0.00%	0.00%	0.00%	0.00%	0.00%	0.00%	0.00%	0.00%	0.00%	0.00%
Aa	Marginal	0.00%	0.00%	0.00%	0.00%	0.00%	0.00%	0.00%	0.00%	0.00%	0.00%
	Cumulative	0.00%	0.00%	0.00%	0.00%	0.00%	0.00%	0.00%	0.00%	0.00%	0.00%
A	Marginal	0.00%	0.00%	0.12%	0.00%	0.00%	0.00%	0.00%	0.00%	0.00%	0.05%
	Cumulative	0.00%	0.00%	0.12%	0.00%	0.12%	0.00%	0.12%	0.00%	0.12%	0.05%
Baa	Marginal	0.04%	0.00%	0.00%	0.00%	0.00%	0.00%	0.00%	0.54%	0.00%	0.00%
	Cumulative	0.04%	0.00%	0.04%	0.00%	0.04%	0.00%	0.04%	0.54%	0.04%	0.54%
Ba	Marginal	0.17%	0.00%	0.60%	0.38%	0.60%	2.30%	0.97%	1.80%	4.89%	0.00%
	Cumulative	0.17%	0.00%	0.77%	0.38%	1.36%	2.67%	2.32%	4.42%	7.10%	4.42%
B	Marginal	2.30%	0.81%	1.86%	1.97%	2.59%	4.99%	1.79%	1.76%	1.86%	0.00%
	Cumulative	2.30%	0.81%	4.11%	2.76%	6.60%	7.61%	8.27%	9.24%	9.97%	9.24%
Caa	Marginal	15.24%	2.65%	7.44%	3.09%	13.03%	4.55%	0.00%	21.72%	0.00%	0.00%
	Cumulative	15.24%	2.65%	21.55%	5.66%	31.77%	9.95%	31.77%	29.51%	31.77%	29.51%

Source: E.I. Altman and H.J. Suggitt, "Default Rates in the Syndicated Loan Market: A Mortality Analysis," Working paper S-97-39, NYU Salomon Center, December 1997.

confidence we have in using the MMR estimate to predict expected losses "out of sample" increases). Because, in any period, a loan or bond either dies or survives,[2] the standard error (σ) of an MMR is:

$$\sigma = \sqrt{MMR_i(1 - MMR_1)/N} \qquad (7.6)$$

and rearranging:

$$N = \frac{MMR_i(1 - MMR_i)}{\sigma^2} \qquad (7.7)$$

As can be seen from equations (7.6) and (7.7), there is an inverse relationship between N (sample size) and the σ (standard error) of a mortality rate estimate.

Suppose that $MMR_1 = .01$ is a mortality rate estimate, and we want to apply extreme actuarial principles of confidence in the stability of the estimate for pricing and prediction out of sample. Extreme actuarial principles might require σ to be one-tenth the size of the mortality rate estimate (or $\sigma = .001$). Plugging the values into equation (7.7), we have:

$$N = \frac{(.01)(.99)}{(.001)^2} = 9,900$$

This suggests that we would need 10,000 loan observations per rating class to get this type of confidence in the estimate. With 10 rating classes (as under most bank rating systems), we would need to analyze a portfolio of some 100,000 loans. With respect to commercial loans, very few banks have built information systems of this type. To get to the requisite large size, a cooperative effort among the banks themselves may be required. The end result of such a cooperative effort might be a National Loan Mortality

---

[2] That is, a mortality rate is binomially distributed [see McAllister and Mingo (1994)] for further discussion.

table that could be as useful in establishing banks' loan loss reserves (based on expected losses) as the National Life Mortality tables are in pricing life insurance.[3]

CSFP CREDIT RISK PLUS

The model developed by CSFP stands in direct contrast to Credit-Metrics in its objectives and its theoretical foundations. Credit-Metrics seeks to estimate the full VAR of a loan or loan portfolio by viewing rating upgrades and downgrades and the associated effects of spread changes in the discount rate as part of the VAR exposure of a loan. Credit Risk Plus views spread risk as part of market risk rather than credit risk. As a result, in any period, only two states of the world are considered—default and no-default—and the focus is on measuring expected and unexpected losses rather than expected value and unexpected changes in value (or VAR) as under CreditMetrics. Thus, CreditMetrics is a mark-to-market (MTM) model; Credit Risk Plus is a default mode (DM) model.

The second major difference is that, in CreditMetrics, the default probability in any year is discrete (as are the upgrade/downgrade probabilities). In Credit Risk Plus, default is modeled as a continuous variable with a probability distribution. An analogy from house fire insurance is relevant. When a whole portfolio of homes is insured, there is a small probability that each house will burn down, and (in general) the probability that each house will burn down can be viewed as an independent event. Similarly, many types of loans, such as mortgages and

---

[3] In most published studies to date, mortality tables have been built on total samples of around 4,000 bonds and loans [see Altman (1989) and Altman and Suggitt (1997)]. However, the Central Bank of Argentina has recently built transition matrices and mortality tables based on over 5 million loan observations. These loan data are available on the Central Bank's Web site.

Figure 7.1   Comparison of Credit Risk Plus and CreditMetrics

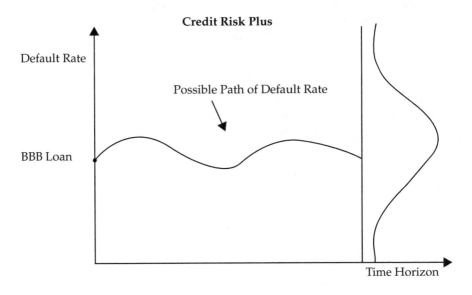

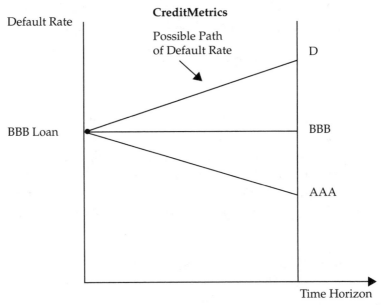

small business loans, can be thought of in the same way, with respect to their default risk. Thus, under Credit Risk Plus, each individual loan is regarded as having a small probability of default, and each loan's probability of default is independent of the default on other loans.[4] This assumption makes the distribution of the default probabilities of a loan portfolio resemble a Poisson distribution. The difference in assumptions regarding default probabilities, between Credit Risk Plus and CreditMetrics, is shown in Figure 7.1.

Default rate uncertainty is only one type of uncertainty modeled in Credit Risk Plus. A second type of uncertainty surrounds the size or severity of the losses themselves. Borrowing again from the fire insurance analogy, when a house "catches fire," the degree of loss severity can vary from the loss of a roof to the complete destruction of the house. In Credit Risk Plus, the fact that severity rates are uncertain is acknowledged, but because of the difficulty of measuring severity on an individual loan-by-loan basis, loss severities or loan exposures are rounded and banded (for example, into discrete $20,000 severity or loss bands). The smaller the bands, the less the degree of inaccuracy that is built into the model as a result of banding.

The two degrees of uncertainty—the frequency of defaults and the severity of losses—produce a distribution of losses for each exposure band. Summing (or accumulating) these losses across exposure bands produces a distribution of losses for the portfolio of loans. Figure 7.2 shows the link between the two types of uncertainty and the distribution of default losses. Although not labeled by CSFP as such, we shall call the model in Figure 7.2 *Model 1*. The computed loss function, assuming the Poisson distribution for individual default rates and the banding

---

[4] This is strictly true for only the simplest of the models in Credit Risk Plus. A more sophisticated version ties loan default probabilities to the systematically varying mean default rate of the "economy" or "sector" of interest.

Figure 7.2   The CSFP Credit Risk Plus Model

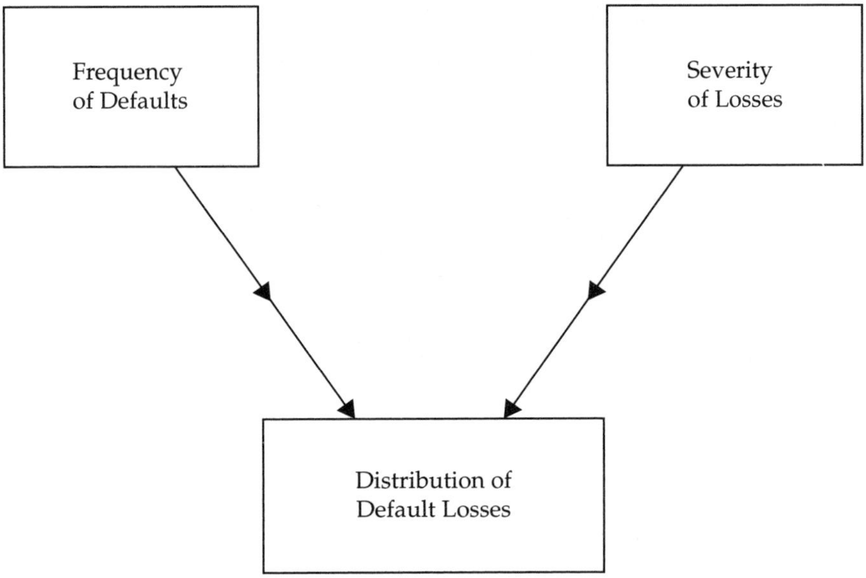

of losses, is shown in Figure 7.3. The loss function is quite "symmetric" and is close to the normal distribution, which it increasingly approximates as the number of loans in the portfolio increases. However, as discussed by CSFP (1997), default rates and loss rates tend to exhibit "fatter tails" than are implied by Figure 7.3. Specifically, the Poisson distribution implies that the mean default rate of a portfolio of loans should equal its variance, that is,

$$\sigma^2 = \text{mean} \tag{7.8}$$

or

$$\sigma = \sqrt{\text{mean}} \tag{7.9}$$

Using figures from Carty and Lieberman (1996) on default rates, CSFP shows that, in general, equation (7.9) does not hold,

Figure 7.3 Distribution of Losses with Default Rate
Uncertainty and Severity Uncertainty

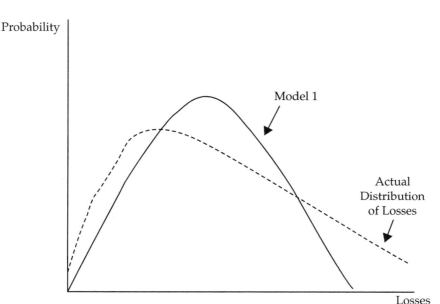

especially for lower-quality credits. For B-rated bonds, Carty and
Lieberman found the mean default rate was 7.27 percent, its
square root was 2.69 percent, and its σ was 5.1 percent, or almost
twice as large as the square root of the mean (see Figure 7.3).

The question is: What extra degree of uncertainty might explain the higher variance (fatter tails) in observed loss distributions? The additional uncertainty modeled by CSFP is that the
mean default rate itself can vary over time (or over the business
cycle). For example, in economic expansions, the mean default rate
will be low; in economic contractions, it may rise significantly. In
their extended model (which we shall call *Model 2*), there are three
types of uncertainty: (1) the uncertainty of the default rate around
any given mean default rate, (2) the uncertainty about the severity

of loss, and (3) the uncertainty about the mean default rate itself [modeled as a gamma distribution by CSFP (1997)].

Appropriately modeled, a loss distribution can be generated along with expected losses and unexpected losses that exhibit observable fatter tails. The latter can then be used to calculate a capital requirement, as shown in Figure 7.4. Note that this economic capital measure is not the same as the VAR measured in Chapter 4 under CreditMetrics because CreditMetrics allows for upgrades and downgrades that affect a loan's value. By contrast, there are no nondefault migrations in the CSFP model. Thus, the CSFP capital measure is closer to a loss-of-earnings or book-value capital measure than a full market value of economic capital measure. Nevertheless, its great advantage is in its parsimonious requirement of

Figure 7.4 Capital Requirement Under the
CSFP Credit Risk Plus Model

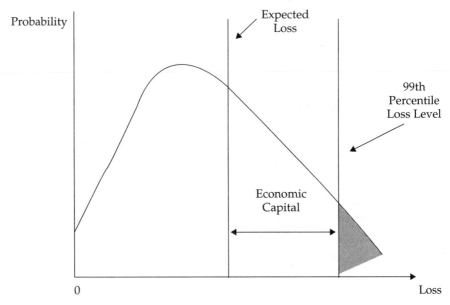

data. The key data inputs are mean loss rates and loss severities, for various bands in the loan portfolio, both of which are potentially amenable to collection, either internally or externally. A simple "discrete" example of the CSFP Model 1 will illustrate the minimal data input that is required.

AN EXAMPLE

Suppose a bank divides its loan portfolio into exposure bands (denoted as v_i by CSFP); that is, it has many different sizes of loans, and each potentially has a different loss exposure. At the lowest end of the exposure levels, it identifies 100 loans, each of which has $20,000 of exposure.[5] One can think of this band ($v = 1$) as containing all loans for which the exposures, when rounded to "the nearest $20,000," are $20,000. The next two exposure bands would represent all loans with a "rounded" exposure of $40,000 ($v = 2$) and $60,000 ($v = 3$), respectively.

As a first step, we want to compute the distribution of losses for the first band. In CSFP Credit Risk Plus, each band can be viewed as a separate portfolio, and the total loss distribution is then an aggregation of the individual loss distributions.

Suppose that, based on historic data, an average of 3 percent of loans with this level of loss exposure ($20,000) default. There are currently 100 loans in the portfolio of this type, so the expected mean default rate *(m)* is 3. However, the actual default rate is uncertain and is assumed to follow a Poisson distribution (see Figure 7.1). Given this assumption, we can compute the

---

[5] The nominal dollar size of these loans can be very different. One loan may have a nominal size of $100,000; another, a nominal size of $25,000. What is similar is the dollar severity of loss on default.

probability of 0 defaults . . . N defaults, and so on, by using the formula for the Poisson distribution:

$$\text{Prob.} \left(n \text{ defaults} \right) = \frac{e^{-m} m^n}{n!} \qquad (7.10)$$

where e = exponential = 2.71828,
   m = mean number of defaults,
   $!$ = factorial,
   n = number of defaults of interest, $n = 1 \ldots N.$

Thus, the probability of 3 defaults is:[6]

$$\text{Prob.} \left(3 \text{ defaults} \right) = \frac{\left(2.71828 \right)^{-3} \times 3^3}{3!}$$

$$= .224$$

and, the probability of 8 defaults is:

$$\text{Prob.} \left(8 \text{ defaults} \right) = \frac{\left(2.71828 \right)^{-3} \times 3^8}{8!}$$

$$= .008$$

The probability that a different number of defaults will occur and the cumulative probability are listed in Table 7.2. The distribution of defaults for band 1 is shown in Figure 7.5. Calculation of the distribution of losses in band 1 is straightforward because, by assumption (and rounding), the loss severity is constant in the v_1 band at $20,000 per loan. Figure 7.6 shows the distribution of losses where the mean number of defaults is 3. The expected loss is then $60,000 in band 1 of the loan portfolio. The 99th percentile (unexpected) loss rate shows slightly less than 8 loans out of 100

---

[6] The term 3! equals $1 \times 2 \times 3 = 6.$

Table 7.2   Calculation of the Probability of Default, Using the Poisson Distribution

N	Probability	Cumulative Probability
0	0.049787	0.049789
1	0.149361	0.199148
2	0.224042	0.42319
3	0.224042	0.647232
•		
•		
•		
8	0.008102	0.996197

Figure 7.5   Distribution of Defaults: Band 1

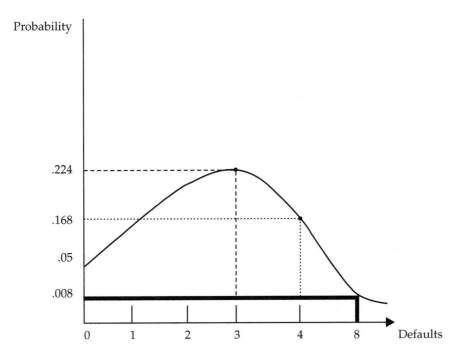

Figure 7.6   Loss Distribution for Single Loan Portfolio.
Severity Rate = $20,000 per $100,000 of Loan

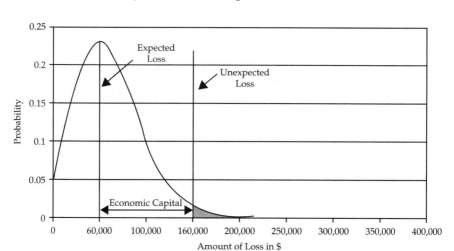

defaulting, which puts the probability of 8 loans defaulting equal
to 0.8 percent. Using 8 loans as an approximation, the 99 percent
unexpected loss rate is $160,000 on portfolio $v = 1$. Viewed in iso-
lation from the rest of the loan portfolio, the capital requirement
would be $100,000 (the unexpected loss minus the expected loss,
or, $160,000 – $60,000).[7] This type of analysis would be repeated
for each loss severity band—$40,000, $60,000, and so on—taking
into account the mean default rates for these higher exposure
bands and then aggregating the band exposures into a total loan
loss distribution.

Continuing the discrete example of a CSFP-type model, suppose, for simplicity, that the band 2 portfolio (v_2), with average
loss exposure of $40,000, also contained 100 loans with a historic
average default rate of 3 percent ($m = 3$). Figure 7.7 shows the loss
distribution for this portfolio. Figure 7.8 shows the aggregation of

_____

[7] Loan loss reserves, if set equal to expected losses, would be $60,000.

Figure 7.7   Single Loan Portfolio. Severity Rate = $40,000 per $100,000 of Loan

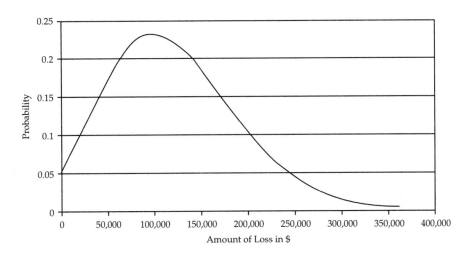

Figure 7.8   Loss Distribution for Two Loan Portfolios with Severity Rates of $20,000 and $40,000

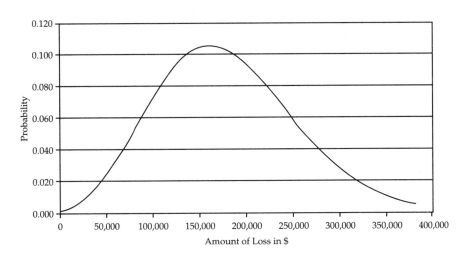

losses across the two portfolio bands, $v = 1$ and $v = 2$. If these were the only types of loans made, this would be the loss distribution for the whole loan portfolio. Notice that, in adding the loan distributions for the two bands, the total loss distribution in Figure 7.8 looks more "normal" than the individual loss distributions for $v = 1$ and $v = 2$.[8]

Finally, this calculation is likely to underestimate the true capital requirement because we assumed the mean default rate was constant in each band. To the extent that mean default rates themselves are variable (e.g., they increase systematically in each band as the "national" default rate increases), the loss distribution will have fatter tails than are implied in this example (and shown in Figure 7.8). Moreover, when the mean default rate in the national economy varies and the default rates in each band are linked to economy-wide default rates, then the default rates in each band can no longer be viewed as independent. (There is a systematic default correlation element among loans; see Chapter 10.)

SUMMARY

In this chapter, we have reviewed two insurance-based approaches to credit risk analysis. Mortality analysis offers an actuarial approach to predicting default rates, which might be thought of

---

[8] In "adding" the two loss distributions, one has to calculate the probabilities by taking into account the possible combination of losses on the two portfolios that might produce some aggregate dollar loss. Thus:

Aggregate Portfolio Loss ($)	(Loss on $v = 1$, Loss on $v = 2$) in $20,000 units	Probability
0	(0, 0)	(.0497 × .0497)
20,000	(1, 0)	(.1493 × .0497)
40,000	[(2, 0) (0, 1)]	[(.224 × .0497) + (.0497 × .1493)]
60,000	[(3, 0) (1, 1)]	[(.224 × .0497) + (.1493)²]
80,000	[(4, 0) (2, 1)(0, 2)]	[(.168 × .0497) + (.224 × .1493) + (.0497 × .224)]
•	•	•
•	•	•
•	•	•

as an alternative to some of the traditional accounting-based models for calculating expected losses and loan loss reserves. However, the predictive usefulness of mortality rates very much depends on the size of the sample of loans/bonds from which they are calculated. Credit Risk Plus, an alternative to Credit-Metrics, calculates capital requirements based on actuarial approaches found in the property insurance literature. Its major advantage is the rather minimal data input required (e.g., no data on credit spreads are required). Its major limitation is that it is not a full VAR model because it concentrates on loss rates rather than loan value changes. It is a default model (DM) rather than a mark-to-market (MTM) model.

Chapter 8

A Summary and Comparison of New Internal Model Approaches

INTRODUCTION

In Chapters 3 through 7, we described key features of some of the more prominent new models of credit risk measurement that are publicly available in complete or partial form. At first sight, these approaches appear to be very different and likely to produce considerably different loan loss exposures and VAR figures. This chapter summarizes four of these new models and discusses key differences and similarities among them. Selected empirical evidence (to date) on predictive differences among these models is very briefly discussed.

MODEL COMPARISON

There are many dimensions along which to compare the new models. We will focus on six key dimensions of four models: (1) CreditMetrics, (2) CreditPortfolioView, (3) Credit Risk Plus, and (4) KMV. Analytically and empirically, these models are not as different as they may first appear. Indeed, similar arguments have been made by Gordy (1998), Koyluoglu and Hickman (1998), and Crouhy and Mark (1998), using different model anatomies.

Table 8.1 lists the six dimensions for comparing the models. Each is discussed here in turn.

Definition of Risk

As described in Chapters 3 through 7, we need to distinguish between models that calculate VAR based on the change in the market value of loans [what the Federal Reserve System Task Force Report (1998) calls mark-to-market (MTM) models], and models that concentrate on predicting default losses [default mode (DM) models]. The MTM models allow for credit upgrades and downgrades (and thus, spread changes) as well as defaults in calculating loan value losses and gains. The DM models consider only two states of the world: default and no-default. As discussed earlier, the key difference between the MTM and DM approaches is the inclusion of spread risk in MTM models. Not surprisingly, if models

Table 8.1   Comparison of Different Approaches

Dimensions for Comparison	Model 1 Credit-Metrics (J.P. Morgan)	Model 2 Credit-PortfolioView (Tom Wilson)	Model 3 Credit Risk Plus (CSFP)	Model 4 KMV
1. Definition of risk	MTM	MTM or DM	DM	MTM or DM
2. Risk drivers	Asset values	Macro factors	Expected default rates	Asset values
3. Volatility of credit events	Constant	Variable	Variable	Variable
4. Correlation of credit events	Multivariate normal asset returns	Factor loadings	Independence assumption or correlation with expected default rate	Multivariate normal asset returns
5. Recovery rates	Random	Random	Constant within band	Constant or random
6. Numerical approach	Simulation or analytic	Simulation	Analytic	Analytic

predict different things, they are likely to produce different results. CreditMetrics is clearly an MTM model. Credit Risk Plus and KMV are essentially DM models. (Although, as will be discussed in Chapter 10, KMV now offers an MTM version.) CreditPortfolio-View can be used as either an MTM or a DM model.

Risk Drivers

At first sight, the key risk drivers of these models appear to be quite different. CreditMetrics and KMV have their analytic foundations in a Merton-type model; a firm's asset values and the volatility of asset values are the key drivers of default risk. In CreditPortfolioView, the risk driver is macro factors (such as the unemployment rate); in Credit Risk Plus, it is the mean level of default risk and its volatility. Yet, if couched in terms of multifactor models, all four models can be viewed as having similar roots.[1] Specifically, the variability of a firm's asset returns in CreditMetrics (as in KMV) is modeled as being directly linked to the variability in a firm's stock returns. In turn, in calculating correlations among firms' asset returns (see Chapter 10), the stocks of individual firms are viewed as being driven by a set of systematic risk factors (industry factors, country factors, and so on) and unsystematic risk factors. The systematic risk factors, along with correlations among systematic risk factors (and their weighted importance), drive the asset returns of individual firms and the default correlations among firms.

The risk drivers in CreditPortfolioView have origins similar to those of CreditMetrics and KMV. In particular, a set of systematic "country-wide" macro factors and unsystematic macro shocks drives default risk and the correlations of default risks among borrowers. The key risk driver in Credit Risk Plus is the variable mean default rate in the economy. This mean default rate can be viewed as being linked systematically to the "state of the macro economy"; when the macro economy deteriorates, the

---

[1] For a good discussion of multifactor models, see Elton and Gruber (1998).

mean default rate is likely to rise, as are default losses. An improvement in economic conditions has the opposite effect.

Thus, the risk drivers and correlations in all four models can be viewed as being linked, to some degree, to a set of macro factors that describe the evolution of economy-wide conditions.

Volatility of Credit Events

A key difference among the models is in the modeling of the one-year default probability or the probability of default distribution function. In CreditMetrics, the probability of default (as well as upgrades and downgrades) is modeled as a fixed or discrete value based on historic data. In KMV, expected default frequencies (EDFs) will vary as new information is impounded in stock prices. Changes in stock prices and the volatility of stock prices underlie KMV's EDF scores. In CreditPortfolioView, the probability of default is a logistic function of a set of macro factors and shocks that are normally distributed; thus, as the macro economy evolves, so will the probability of default and the cells, or probabilities, in the rest of the transition matrix. In Credit Risk Plus, the probability of each loan's defaulting is viewed as variable and conforming to a Poisson distribution around some mean default rate. In turn, the mean default rate is modeled as a variable with a gamma distribution. This produces a distribution of losses that may have "fatter tails" than those produced by either CreditMetrics or CreditPortfolioView.

Correlation of Credit Events

The similarity of the determinants of credit risk correlations has already been discussed in the context of risk drivers. Specifically, the correlation structure in all four models can be linked to systematic linkages of loans to key factors. The correlations among borrowers will be discussed in greater length in Chapters 9 through 11, where the application of the new models, and modern portfolio theory, to the credit portfolio decision is analyzed.

Recovery Rates

The distribution of losses and VAR calculations depend not only on the probability of defaults but also on the severity of losses or loss given default (LGD). Empirical evidence suggests that default severities and recoveries are quite volatile over time. Further, building in a volatile recovery rate is likely to increase the VAR or unexpected loss rate. (See, for example, the discussion on CreditMetrics in Chapter 4.)

CreditMetrics, in the context of its VAR calculations, allows for recoveries to be variable. In the normal distribution version of the model, the estimated standard deviation of recoveries is built into the VAR calculation. In the "actual" distribution version, which recognizes a skew in the tail of the loan value loss distribution function, recoveries are assumed to follow a beta distribution, and the VAR of loans is calculated via a Monte Carlo simulation. In KMV's simplest model, recoveries are viewed as a constant. In more recent extended versions of the model, recoveries are allowed to follow a beta distribution as well. In Credit-PortfolioView, recoveries are also estimated via a Monte Carlo simulation approach. By contrast, under Credit Risk Plus, loss severities are rounded and banded into subportfolios, and the loss severity in any subportfolio is viewed as a constant.

Numerical Approach

The numerical approach to estimation of VARs, or unexpected losses, also differs across models. A VAR, at both the individual-loan level and the portfolio-of-loans level, can be calculated analytically under CreditMetrics, but this approach becomes increasingly intractable as the number of loans in the portfolio increases. (This is discussed in more detail in Chapter 10.) As a result, for large loan portfolios, Monte Carlo simulation techniques are used to generate an "approximate" aggregate distribution of portfolio loan values, and hence a VAR. Similarly, CreditPortfolioView uses repeated Monte Carlo simulations to generate macro shocks and the distribution of losses (or loan values) on a loan portfolio. By comparison, Credit Risk Plus, based on its convenient distributional assumptions (the Poisson distribution for individual loans and the gamma distribution for the mean default rate, along with the fixed recovery assumption for loan losses in each subportfolio of loans), allows an analytic or closed-form solution to be generated for the probability density function of losses. KMV also allows an analytic solution to the loss function.

EMPIRICAL SIMULATIONS

Given the relative newness of these models, it is not surprising that only a few direct comparison studies have been conducted to date.[2] The usual approach has been to make the definition of risk and the assumption about recoveries common, and to concentrate on modeling the effects of other assumptions on the loss distributions. In particular, in comparison studies all four models analyzed are usually assumed to be estimating loss distributions and unexpected loss rates rather than full VAR (i.e., to use a DM rather than MTM), and recovery rates are viewed as constants. In this context, Gordy (1998), using data from Carey (1998) and from the Society of Actuaries (1996) study of insurance companies' privately placed bond portfolios and portfolio losses from 1986 to 1992, compared CreditMetrics with Credit Risk Plus and found that the constrained form of CreditMetrics produced unexpected loss values similar to those of Credit Risk Plus, as long as the volatility (σ) of the mean default rate (systematic risk factor) followed its historically estimated value. However, for extremely large values of the volatility of the mean default rate, the unexpected loss figures of the two models began to diverge. This occurred because of (1) the greater kurtotic

---

[2] The ISDA has sponsored a project to evaluate the different models. At the time of publication, the ISDA had yet to report its findings.

nature of the loss tails under the Credit Risk Plus model and (2) the fact that the kurtosis and fat tailedness of Credit Risk Plus directly depend on the value of σ.

Koyluoglu and Hickman (1998) conducted a study on the default mode (DM) versions of three models with fixed recovery rates. Using a statistic that measured the degree of agreement in the tails ($\bar{p} + 2\sigma$ to infinity) of default rate distributions, they found that the degree of similarity depended crucially on the extent to which they harmonized key parameter values across the three models (CreditMetrics, CreditPortfolioView, and Credit Risk Plus). In particular, "unsurprisingly, when the parameters do not imply consistent mean and standard deviation of default rate distribution, the result is that the models are significantly different" (p. 15).

Crouhy and Mark (1998) compared CreditMetrics (DM version) and Credit Risk Plus with KMV and (CIBC's) Canadian Imperial Bank of Commerce's own internal model (Credit VAR 1). Examining a diversified portfolio of more than 1,800 bonds across 13 currencies and a whole spectrum of qualities and maturities, they found that unexpected losses fall in a quite narrow range.

SUMMARY

The development of internal models for credit risk measurement is at an early stage. In some sense, its present level of development is similar to that of market risk in 1994, when RiskMetrics first appeared and was followed by alternative approaches such as historic simulation and Monte Carlo simulation. The credit risk models publicly available to date have exhibited quite different characteristics across a number of important dimensions. Harmonizing these models across just a few key dimensions, however, can result in quite similar unexpected loss projections. This is reassuring and suggests that, in time, with theoretical and model development, a consensus model or approach may eventually emerge. To some extent, this has already happened in the market risk modeling area.

Chapter **9**

An Overview of Modern Portfolio Theory and Its Application to Loan Portfolios

Introduction

So far, we have considered default-risk and credit-risk exposure on a single-borrower basis. This is not unreasonable; much of the banking theory literature views the personnel at banks and similar FIs as credit specialists who, through monitoring and the development of long-term relationships with customers, gain a comparative advantage in lending to a specific borrower or group of borrowers.[1]

This advantage, developed by making (and holding to maturity) loans to a select subset of long-term borrowers, may nevertheless be inefficient from a risk–return perspective. Suppose, instead, loans were publicly traded (or were "swappable" with other FIs) and could be viewed as being similar to "commodity"-type assets such as equities, which are freely traded at low transaction costs and with high liquidity in public securities markets. By separating the credit-granting decision from the credit portfolio decision, a bank may be able to generate a better risk–return

---

[1] Moreover, the BIS risk-based capital ratio is linearly additive across individual loans. See Rajan (1992) for an example of the "customer relationship" model.

trade-off and offset what KMV and others have called the "paradox of credit."

In Figure 9.1, which illustrates the paradox of credit, portfolio A is a relatively concentrated loan portfolio for a traditional bank that makes and monitors loans, and holds those loans to maturity. Portfolios B and C are on the "efficient frontier" of loan portfolios. They achieve either the maximum return for any level of risk (B) or the minimum risk for a given return (C). To move from A to either B or C, the bank must actively manage its loan portfolio in a manner similar to the tenets of modern portfolio theory (MPT), where the key focus for improving the risk–return trade-off is on (1) the (default) correlations among the assets held in the

Figure 9.1   The Paradox of Credit

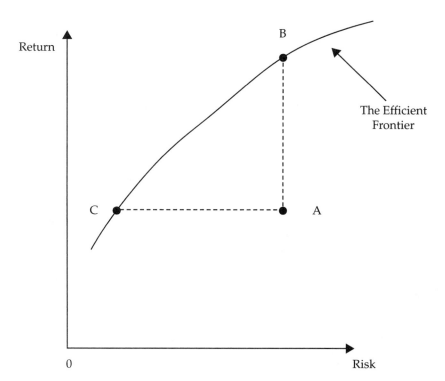

portfolio and (2) a willingness, as market conditions change, to flexibly adjust the amount of different assets held, rather than to make and hold loans to maturity, as is the practice under traditional relationship banking.

In this chapter, we first describe the main features of MPT and then raise important issues regarding applications of MPT to nontraded loans and bonds.

MPT: An Overview

The (mean) return and risk of a portfolio of assets, under the assumption that returns on individual assets are normally distributed (or that asset managers have a quadratic utility function), are given in equations (9.1), (9.2), and (9.3). An assumption either that individual asset returns are normally distributed or that managers of an FI exhibit a particular set of preferences (quadratic utility) toward returns implies that only two moments of the distribution of assets returns are necessary in order to analyze portfolio decisions: (1) the mean return of a portfolio and (2) its variance (or the standard deviation of the returns on that portfolio). MPT itself, being based on expected returns and risks, is forward-looking; these, by definition, are unobservable. As a result, portfolio returns and risks are usually estimated from historic time series of the returns and risks on individual assets.

Given these assumptions, the mean return on a portfolio of assets $(\overline{R}_p)$ and the variance of returns (σ_p^2) on a portfolio of assets can be computed as:

$$\overline{R}_p = \sum_{i=1}^{n} X_i \overline{R}_i \tag{9.1}$$

$$\sigma_p^2 = \sum_{i=1}^{N} X_i^2 \sigma_i^2 + \sum_{i=1}^{N} \sum_{\substack{j=1 \\ i \neq j}}^{N} X_i X_j \sigma_{ij} \tag{9.2}$$

or

$$\sigma_p^2 = \sum_{i=1}^{N} X_i^2 \sigma_i^2 + \sum_{i=1}^{N} \sum_{\substack{j=1 \\ i \neq j}}^{N} X_i X_j \rho_{ij} \sigma_i \sigma_j \qquad (9.3)$$

where $\overline{R}_p$ = the mean return on the asset portfolio,

Σ = summation,

$\overline{R}_i$ = the mean return on the ith asset in the portfolio,

X_i = the proportion of the asset portfolio invested in the ith asset,

σ_i^2 = the variance of returns on the ith asset,

σ_{ij} = the covariance of returns between the ith and jth assets,

ρ_{ij} = the correlation between the returns on the ith and jth assets and $-1 \leq \rho_{ij} \leq +1$.

From equation (9.1), the mean return on a portfolio of assets $(\overline{R}_p)$ is simply a weighted (X_i) sum of the mean returns on the individual assets in that portfolio $(\overline{R}_i)$. By comparison, the variance of returns on a portfolio of assets (σ_p^2) is decomposable into two terms. The first term reflects the weighted (X_i^2) sum of the variances of returns on the individual assets (σ_i^2), and the second term reflects the weighted sums of the covariances among the assets (σ_{ij}). Because a covariance is unbounded, it is common in MPT-type models to substitute the correlation among asset returns for the covariance term, using the statistical definition:

$$\sigma_{ij} = \rho_{ij} \sigma_i \sigma_j \qquad (9.4)$$

Because a correlation is constrained to lie between plus and minus unity, we can evaluate the effect of ρ_{ij} varying on asset portfolio risk. For example, in the two-asset case, if ρ_{ij} is negative, the second term in equation (9.3) will also be negative and will offset the first term, which will always be positive.[2] By appropriately

---

[2] See Elton and Gruber (1998) for proofs.

exploiting correlation relationships among assets, a portfolio manager can significantly reduce risk and improve a portfolio's risk–return trade-off (which, in the context of Figure 9.1, is to move the portfolio from A to B or C). Computationally, the efficient frontier, or the portfolio of assets with the lowest risk for any given level of return, can be calculated by solving for the asset proportions (X_i) that minimize σ_p for each given level of returns $(\overline{R}_p)$. Both B and C are efficient asset portfolios in this sense.

The best of all the risky asset portfolios on the efficient frontier is the one that exhibits the highest excess return over the risk-free rate (r_f) relative to the level of portfolio risk, or the highest risk-adjusted excess return:

$$\frac{\overline{R}_p - r_f}{\sigma_p} \qquad (9.5)$$

This risk–return ratio is usually called the *Sharpe ratio*. Diagrammatically, the optimal risky asset portfolio is the one in which a line drawn from the return axis, with an origin at r_f, is just tangential to the efficient frontier (this is shown as portfolio D in Figure 9.2). Because the slope of this line reflects the $(\overline{R}_p - r_f)/\sigma_p$ ratio for that portfolio, it is also the portfolio with the highest Sharpe ratio.[3]

APPLYING MPT TO NONTRADED BONDS AND LOANS

MPT has been around for over 40 years and is now a portfolio management tool commonly used by most mutual fund and pension fund managers. It has also been applied with some success to publicly traded junk bonds when their returns have tended to be more equitylike than bondlike and when historical returns are available [see Altman and Saunders (1997)]. With respect to most

---

[3] It might be noted that in identifying point D, it is assumed that investors (FIs) can borrow and lend at the same (risk-free) rate.

Figure 9.2   The Optimum Risky Loan Portfolio

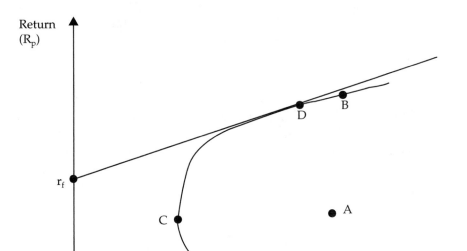

$$D = \text{the portfolio with the highest Sharpe ratio: } \frac{(\overline{R}_p - r_f)}{\sigma_p}.$$

loans and bonds, however, there are problems with nonnormal returns, unobservable returns, and unobservable correlations.

Nonnormal Returns

As discussed in Chapters 3 and 4, loans and bonds tend to have relatively fixed upside returns and long-tailed downside risks. Thus, returns on these assets tend to exhibit a strong negative skew and, in some cases, kurtosis (fat-tailedness) as well. MPT is built around a model in which only two moments—the mean and variance—are required to describe the whole distribution of returns. To the extent that the third (skew) and fourth (kurtosis) moments of returns are material in fully describing the distribution of asset returns, the use of simple, two moment, MPT models becomes difficult to justify.[4]

Unobservable Returns

A further problem relates to the fact that most loans and corporate bonds are nontraded or are traded over-the-counter at very uneven intervals with little historical price or volume data. This makes it difficult to compute mean returns $(\overline{R}_i)$ and the variance of returns (σ_i^2) using historic time series.

Unobservable Correlations

Relatedly, if price and return data are unavailable, calculating the covariance (σ_{ij}) or correlation (ρ_{ij}) among asset returns also becomes difficult. Yet, as discussed above, these correlations are a key building block in MPT-type analysis.

SUMMARY

MPT provides an extremely useful framework for a loan portfolio manager considering risk–return trade-offs. The lower the correlation among loans in a portfolio, the greater the potential for a manager to reduce a bank's risk exposure through diversification. Further, to the extent that a VAR-based capital requirement reflects the concentration risk and default correlations of the loan portfolio, such a portfolio may have lower credit risk than when loan exposures are considered independently additive (as under the current BIS 8 percent capital ratio).

---

[4] Although, arguably, as the number of loans in a portfolio gets bigger, the distribution of returns tends to become more "normal."

Unfortunately, there are a number of problems in applying MPT to loans (and many bonds)—in particular, the nonnormality of loan returns and the unobservability of market-based loan returns (and, thus, correlations) as a result of the fact that most loans are "nontraded." In the next chapter, we will examine portfolio models suggested by KMV, CreditMetrics, and others in an attempt to overcome these problems. Specific attention will be given to how these new models calculate returns, risk, and correlations on loans and loan portfolios.

Chapter 10

Loan Portfolio Selection and Risk Measurement

INTRODUCTION

In this chapter, we will look at a number of applications of MPT-type techniques to the loan portfolio. We will distinguish between models that seek to calculate the full risk–return trade-off for a portfolio of loans (such as KMV's Portfolio Manager) and models that can be viewed as concentrating mostly on the risk dimension (such as CreditMetrics) and the VAR of the loan portfolio.[1]

KMV's PORTFOLIO MANAGER

KMV's Portfolio Manager can be viewed as a full-fledged MPT optimization approach because all three key variables—returns, risks, and correlations—are calculated. However, it can also be used to analyze risk effects alone, as will be discussed below. This section explains how the three key variables that enter into any MPT model can be calculated.

---

[1] The RiskMetrics Group is currently adding a return dimension to Credit-Metrics.

Returns

In the absence of historic returns on traded loans, the (expected) return on the ith loan (R_{it}) over any given horizon can be set equal to:

$$R_{it} = [\text{Spread}_i + \text{Fees}_i] - [\text{Expected loss}_i] \qquad (10.1)$$

or:

$$R_{it} = [\text{Spread}_i + \text{Fees}_i] - [\text{EDF}_i \times \text{LGD}_i] \qquad (10.2)$$

The first component of returns is the spread of the loan rate over a benchmark rate such as the London Inter-Bank Offered Rate (LIBOR), plus any fees directly earned from the loan and expected over a given period (say, a year). Expected losses on the loan are then deducted because they can be viewed as part of the "normal cost" of doing banking business. In the context of a KMV-type model, where the expected default frequency (EDF) is calculated from stock returns (the Credit Monitor Model), then, for any given borrower, expected losses will equal $\text{EDF}_i \times \text{LGD}_i$, where LGD_i is the loss given default for the ith borrower (usually estimated from the bank's internal data-base).

Loan Risks

In the absence of return data on loans, a loan's risk (σ_i) can be approximated by the unexpected loss rate on the loan (UL_i)—essentially, the variability of the loss rate around its expected value ($\text{EDF}_i \times \text{LGD}_i$). There are a number of ways in which UL_i might be calculated, depending on the assumptions made about the number of credit quality transitions, the variability of LGD, and the correlation of LGDs with EDFs. For example, in the simplest form, we can assume a DM model where the borrower either defaults or doesn't default, so that defaults are binomially distributed and LGD is fixed across all borrowers. Then:

$$\sigma_i = \text{UL}_i = \sqrt{(\text{EDF}_i)(1 - \text{EDF}_i)} \times \text{LGD} \qquad (10.3)$$

where $\sqrt{(EDF_i)(1 - EDF_i)}$ reflects the variability of a default rate frequency that is binomially distributed. A slightly more sophisticated DM version would allow LGD_i to be variable, but factors affecting EDFs are assumed to be different from those affecting LGDs, and LGDs are assumed to be independent across borrowers. In this case [see Kealhofer (1995)]:

$$\sigma_i = \sqrt{EDF_i(1 - EDF_i)\overline{LGD}_i^{\,2} + EDF_i VOL_i^{\,2}} \qquad (10.4)$$

where VOL_i is the standard deviation of borrower i's LGD. If we want to develop σ_i measures, allowing for a full MTM model with credit upgrades and downgrades as well as default, then σ_i might be calculated similar to CreditMetrics, as discussed later. Indeed, in recent versions of its model, KMV produces a rating transition matrix based on EDFs and allow for a full MTM calculation of σ_i to be made.[2]

Correlations

One important intuition from a KMV-type approach is that default correlations are likely to be low. To see why, consider the context of the two-state DM version of a KMV-type model. A default correlation would reflect the joint probability of two firms Y and X—say, for example, General Motors and Ford—having their asset values fall below their debt values over the same horizon (say, 1 year). In the context of Figure 10.1, the General Motors asset value would have to fall below its debt value (B_Y) in Figure 10.1, and the Ford asset value would have to fall below its debt value (B_X). The joint area of default is shaded, and the joint probability distribution of asset values are represented by the iso-circles. The iso-circles are similar to those used in geography charts to describe hills. The inner circle is the top of the hill (high probability), and the outer circles are the bottom of the hill (low

---

[2] The EDFs of KMV vary from 0% to 20%. By breaking EDF's into score ranges or categories a transition matrix can be generated based on EDF scores.

Figure 10.1   Joint Default Probabilities: KMV Portfolio Manager

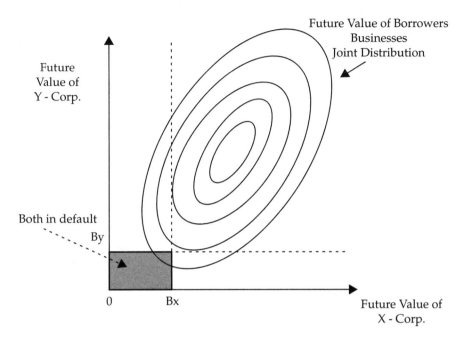

Source: "Modeling Portfolio Risk," KMV Corporation © 1997.

probability). The joint probability that asset values will fall in the shaded region is low and will depend, in part, on the asset correlations between the two borrowers. In the context of the simple binomial model [for Ford (F) and General Motors (G)]:

$$\rho_{GF} = \frac{COV_{GF}}{SD_F \times SD_G} \tag{10.5}$$

or:

$$\rho_{GF} = \frac{JDF_{GF} - \left(EDF_G \times EDF_F\right)}{\sqrt{\left(EDF_G\right)\left(1 - EDF_G\right)} \cdot \sqrt{\left(EDF_F\right)\left(1 - EDF_F\right)}} \tag{10.6}$$

The numerator of equation (10.6) is the covariance (COV_{GF}) between the asset values of the two firms, G and F. It reflects the difference between when the two asset values are jointly distributed (JDF_{GF}) and when they are independent ($EDF_G \times EDF_F$). The denominator reflects the standard deviation (SD) of default rates under the binomial distribution for each firm.

Rather than seeking to directly estimate correlations using equation (10.6), KMV uses a multifactor stock-return model from which correlations are derived. The model reflects the correlation among the systematic risk factors affecting each firm and their appropriate weights. Because KMV's approach to calculating correlations is somewhat similar to the CreditMetrics approach, we will discuss the stock-return factor approach to correlation calculation more fully later in this chapter. However, KMV typically finds that correlations lie in the range .002 to .15.

After they are calculated, the three inputs (returns, risks, and correlations) can be employed in a number of directions. One potential use would be to calculate a risk-return efficient frontier for the loan portfolio, as discussed in Chapter 9. Reportedly, one large Canadian bank manages its U.S. loan portfolio using a KMV-type model.[3]

A second use would be to measure the risk contribution of expanding lending to any given borrower. As discussed in Chapter 9, the risk (in a portfolio sense) of any one loan will depend on the risk of the individual loan on a stand-alone basis, and its correlation with the risks of other loans. For example, a loan, when viewed individually, might be thought to be risky, but because its returns are negatively correlated with other loans, it may be quite valuable in a "portfolio" context in constraining or lowering portfolio risk.

The effects of making additional loans to a particular borrower also depend crucially on assumptions made about the

---

[3] It is used for U.S. loans because "customer relationships" are weaker for its U.S. borrowers than for its Canadian borrowers; i.e., U.S. loans can be viewed as being more commoditized for this bank.

balance sheet constraint. For example, if investable or loanable funds are viewed as fixed, then expanding the proportion of assets lent to any borrower i (i.e., increasing X_i) means reducing the proportion invested in all other loans (assets). However, if the funds constraint is viewed as being nonbinding, then the amount lent to borrower i can be expanded without affecting the amount lent to other borrowers. In the KMV-type marginal risk contribution calculation, a funding constraint is assumed to be binding:

$$X_i + X_j + \ldots\ldots + X_n = 1$$

By comparison, under CreditMetrics (see the next section), marginal risk contributions are calculated assuming no such funding constraint; for example, a bank can make a loan to a twentieth borrower without reducing the loans outstanding to the nineteen other borrowers.

Assuming a binding funding constraint, the marginal risk contribution for the ith loan (MRC_i) can be calculated as:

$$\text{MRC}_i = X_i \frac{d\text{UL}_p}{dX_i} \tag{10.7}$$

where UL_p is the risk of the total loan portfolio and X_i is the proportion of the loan portfolio made to the ith borrower:

$$\text{UL}_p = \left[\sum_{i=1}^{N} X_i^2 \text{UL}_i^2 + \sum_{i=1}^{N} \sum_{\substack{j=1 \\ i \neq j}}^{N} X_i X_j \text{UL}_i \text{UL}_j \rho_{ij} \right]^{\frac{1}{2}} \tag{10.8}$$

and

$$\sum_{i=1}^{N} X_i = 1 \tag{10.9}$$

The marginal risk contribution can be viewed as a measure of the economic capital needed by the bank in order to make a new loan to the *i*th borrower because it reflects the sensitivity of portfolio risk (specifically, portfolio standard deviation) to a small percentage change in the weight of the asset. Note that the sum of MRCs is equal to UL*p*; consequently, the required capital for each loan is just its MRC scaled by the capital multiple (the ratio of capital to UL*p*).[4]

CreditMetrics

Unlike KMV, CreditMetrics can be viewed more as a loan portfolio risk-minimizing model than a full-fledged MPT risk–return model. Specifically, returns on loans are not explicitly modeled. Here, we will concentrate on the measurement of the VAR for a loan portfolio. As with individual loans, two approaches to measuring VAR are considered:

1. Loans are assumed to have normally distributed asset values.

2. The actual distribution exhibits a long-tailed downside or negative skew.

We will first consider the normal distribution case, which produces a direct analytic solution to VAR calculations using conventional MPT techniques.

CreditMetrics: Portfolio VAR Under the Normal Distribution

In the normal distribution model, a two-loan case provides a useful benchmark. A two-loan case is readily generalizable to the *N*-loan case; that is, the risk of a portfolio of *N* loans can be shown to depend on the risk of each pair of loans in the portfolio (see the later discussion and the Appendix to this chapter).

To calculate the VAR of a portfolio of two loans, we need to calculate: (1) the joint migration probabilities for each loan (assumed

---

[4] In recent presentations, KMV has been using a multiple of 10. That is, Capital = UL*p* × 10.

to be the $100-million face value BBB loan discussed in Chapter 4, and an A-rated loan of $100 million face value) and (2) the joint payoffs or values of the loans for each possible one-year joint migration probability.

Joint Migration Probabilities

Table 10.1 shows the one-year individual and joint migration probabilities for the BBB and A loans. Given 8 possible credit states for the BBB borrower and 8 possible credit states for the A borrower over the next year (the one-year horizon), there are 64 joint migration probabilities. (See the cells of Table 10.1.) Importantly, the joint migration probabilities are not simply the product of the two individual migration probabilities. This can be seen by looking at the independent probabilities that the BBB loan will remain BBB (.8693) and the A loan will remain single A (.9105) over the next year. The joint probability, assuming the correlation between the two migration probabilities is zero, would be:

$$.8693 \times .9105 = .7915 \text{ or } 79.15 \text{ percent.}$$

Table 10.1   Joint Migration Probabilities with 0.30 Asset Correlation (%)

Obligor 1 (BBB)		Obligor 2 (A)							
		AAA	AA	A	BBB	BB	B	CCC	Default
		0.09	2.27	91.05	5.52	0.74	0.26	0.01	0.06
AAA	0.02	0.00	0.00	0.02	0.00	0.00	0.00	0.00	0.00
AA	0.33	0.00	0.04	0.29	0.00	0.00	0.00	0.00	0.00
A	5.95	0.02	0.39	5.44	0.08	0.01	0.00	0.00	0.00
BBB	86.93	0.07	1.81	79.69	4.55	0.57	0.19	0.01	0.04
BB	5.30	0.00	0.02	4.47	0.64	0.11	0.04	0.00	0.01
B	1.17	0.00	0.00	0.92	0.18	0.04	0.02	0.00	0.00
CCC	0.12	0.00	0.00	0.09	0.02	0.00	0.00	0.00	0.00
Default	0.18	0.00	0.00	0.13	0.04	0.01	0.00	0.00	0.00

Source: CREDITMETRICS-Technical Document, April 2, 1997, p. 38.

Note that the joint probability in Table 10.1 is slightly higher, at 79.69 percent, because the (assumed) correlation is .3 between the two borrowers.

Adjusting the migration table to reflect correlations is a two-step process. First, a model is needed to explain migration transitions. In CreditMetrics, a Merton-type model is used to link asset value or return volatility to discrete rating migrations for individual borrowers. Second, a model is needed to calculate the correlations among the asset value volatilities of individual borrowers. Similar to KMV, asset values of borrowers are unobservable, as are correlations among those asset values. The correlations among the individual borrowers are therefore estimated from multifactor models driving borrowers' stock returns.

An Example of the Link Between Asset Volatilities and Rating Transitions

To see the link between asset volatilities and rating transitions, consider Figure 10.2, which links standardized normal asset

Figure 10.2   The Link between Asset Value Volatility (σ) and Rating Transitions for a BB-Rated Borrower

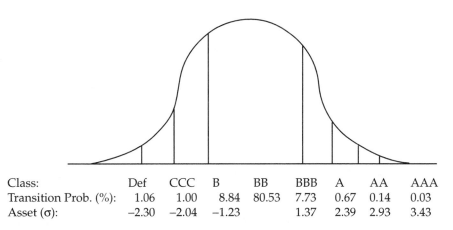

Class:	Def	CCC	B	BB	BBB	A	AA	AAA
Transition Prob. (%):	1.06	1.00	8.84	80.53	7.73	0.67	0.14	0.03
Asset (σ):	−2.30	−2.04	−1.23		1.37	2.39	2.93	3.43

Table 10.2   The Link Between Asset Value Volatility (σ) and Rating Transitions for an A-Rated Borrower

Class	Default	CCC	B	BB	BBB	A	AA	AAA
Trans. Prob.	0.06	0.01	0.26	0.74	5.52	91.05	2.27	0.09
Asset (σ)	−3.24	−3.19	−2.72	−2.30	−1.51		1.98	3.12

return changes (measured in standard deviations) of a BB-rated borrower to rating transitions.[5] If the unobservable (standardized) changes in asset values of the firm are assumed to be normally distributed, we can calculate how many standard deviations asset values would have to have to change to move the firm from BB into default. For example, the historic one-year default probability of this type of BB borrower is 1.06 percent. Using the standardized normal distribution tables, asset values would have to fall by 2.3σ for the firm to default. Also, there is a 1 percent probability that the BB firm will move to a C rating over the year. Asset values would have to fall by at least 2.04σ to change the BB borrower's rating to C or below.[6] The full range of possibilities is graphed in Figure 10.2. Similar figures could be constructed for a BBB borrower, an A borrower, and so on. The links between asset volatility and rating changes for an A borrower are shown in Table 10.2.

From Figure 10.2, we can see that a BB-rated borrower will remain BB as long as the standardized normal asset returns of the borrowing firm fluctuate between -1.23σ and $+1.37\sigma$. The A borrower's rating will remain unchanged as long as the asset returns of the firm vary within the -1.51σ and $+1.98\sigma$ range. Assume that the correlation (ρ) between those two firms' asset returns is .2 (to

---

[5] A standardized return is an actual return that is divided by its estimated standard deviation after subtracting the mean return. Thus, a standardized normal distribution has a mean of zero and a standard deviation of unity.

[6] There is a 2.06 percent probability (1.06 percent + 1.00 percent) that the BB-rated borrower will be downgraded to C or below (such as D).

be calculated in more detail below). The joint probability (Pr) that both borrowers will remain in the same rating class during the next year can be found by integrating the bivariate normal density function[7] as follows:

$$Pr(-1.23 < BB < 1.37, -1.51 < A < 1.98) = \int_{-1.23}^{1.37} \int_{-1.51}^{1.98} f(Y_1 Y_2; \rho) \, dY_2 dY_1$$

$$= .7365 \tag{10.10}$$

where Y_1 and Y_2 are random, and $\rho = 0.20$.

In equation (10.10), the ρ_i (correlation coefficient's value) was assumed to be equal to .2. As described next, these correlations, in general, are calculated in CreditMetrics from multifactor models of stock returns for individual borrowers.[8]

An Example of Correlation Calculation

Consider two firms, A and Z. We do not observe their asset values or returns, but we do observe their stock returns. Both are publicly traded companies. The returns (R_A) on stocks of company A, a chemical company, are driven by a single industry index factor (R_{CHEM}, the returns on the chemical industry index) and some idiosyncratic risk (U_A) assumed to be diversifiable in a portfolio context. The estimated sensitivity of firm A's returns to the chemical industry's returns is .9. Thus:[9]

$$R_A = .9R_{CHEM} + U_A \tag{10.11}$$

Firm Z can be considered a universal bank. It has return sensitivity to two factors: the German banking industry return index

---

[7] J.P. Morgan and other vendors offer software to do this function.

[8] Arguably, we should be measuring correlations between loans and not borrowers. For example, a low quality borrower with a highly secured loan would find the loan rated more highly than the borrower as a whole.

[9] CreditMetrics requires the user to input the sensitivity coefficients him or herself.

(R_{BANK}) and the German insurance industry return index (R_{INS}). The estimated independent sensitivities are, respectively, .15 and .74. Thus:

$$R_z = .74R_{INS} + .15R_{BANK} + U_Z \qquad (10.12)$$

The correlation between the two firms, A and Z, will depend on the correlation between the chemical industry return index and the insurance industry return index and on the correlation between the chemical industry index and the banking industry index:[10]

$$\rho(A,Z) = [(.9)(.74)(\rho_{CHEM,INS}) + (.9)(.15)(\rho_{CHEM,BANK})] \qquad (10.13)$$

If the correlations $\rho_{CHEM,INS}$ and $\rho_{CHEM,BANK}$ are, respectively, .16 and .08, we have:

$$\rho(A,Z) = [(.9)(.74)(.16) + (.9)(.15)(.08)]$$

$$\rho(A,Z) = [.1066 + .0108] = .1174$$

Firms A and Z have a low but positive default correlation, and correlation values calculated in a similar fashion are inserted into equation (10.10) to solve the bivariate normal density function and, thus, the joint migration probability in tables such as Table 10.1.

Joint Loan Values

In addition to 64 joint migration probabilities, we can calculate 64 joint loan values in the two-loan case. The market value for each loan in each credit state is calculated as in Chapter 4. Individual

---

[10] By construction of the factor sensitivities, the bank and insurance indexes are independent of each other. Note the correlation among the unsystematic return components: U_A and U_Z are zero by assumption.

loan values are then added to get a portfolio loan value, as shown in Table 10.3. Thus, if, over the year, both loans get upgraded to AAA, then the market value of the loan portfolio at the one-year horizon becomes $215.96 million. By comparison, if both loans default, the value of the loan portfolio becomes $102.26 million.

With 64 possible joint probabilities and 64 possible loan values, the mean value of the portfolio and its variance are as computed in equations (10.14) and (10.15):

$$\text{Mean} = p_1 \cdot V_1 + p_2 \cdot V_2 + \ldots + p_{64} \cdot V_{64}$$
$$= \$213.63 \text{ million} \tag{10.14}$$

$$
\begin{aligned}
\text{Variance} = {} & p_1 \cdot (V_1 - \text{Mean})^2 \\
& + p_2 \cdot (V_2 - \text{Mean})^2 + \ldots \\
& + p_{64} \cdot (V_{64} - \text{Mean})^2 \\
= {} & \$11.22 \text{ million}^2
\end{aligned}
\tag{10.15}
$$

Table 10.3   Loan Portfolio Values

		All Possible 64 Year-End Values for a Two-Loan Portfolio ($)							
		Obligor 2 (single-A)							
Obligor 1 (BBB)		AAA	AA	A	BBB	BB	B	CCC	Default
		106.59	106.49	106.30	105.64	103.15	101.39	88.71	51.13
AAA	109.37	215.96	215.86	215.67	215.01	212.52	210.76	198.08	160.50
AA	109.19	215.78	215.68	215.49	214.83	212.34	210.58	197.90	160.32
A	108.66	215.25	215.15	214.96	214.30	211.81	210.05	197.37	159.79
BBB	107.55	214.14	214.04	<u>213.85</u>	213.19	210.70	208.94	196.26	158.68
BB	102.02	208.61	208.51	208.33	207.66	205.17	203.41	190.73	153.15
B	98.10	204.69	204.59	<u>204.40</u>	203.74	210.25	199.49	186.81	149.23
CCC	83.64	190.23	190.13	189.94	189.28	186.79	185.03	172.35	134.77
Default	51.13	157.72	157.62	157.43	156.77	154.28	152.52	139.84	102.26

Source: CREDITMETRICS-Technical Document, April 2, 1997, p. 12.

Taking the square root of the solution to equation (10.15), the σ of the loan portfolio value is $3.35 million and the 99 percent VAR under the normal distribution is:

$$2.33 \times \$3.35 = \$7.81 \text{ million} \qquad (10.16)$$

Interestingly, comparing this value of $7.81 million, for a (face value) loan portfolio of $200 million, with the 99 percent VAR-based capital requirement of $6.97 million, for the single BBB loan of $100 million in Chapter 4, we can see that although the loan portfolio has doubled in face value, a VAR-based capital requirement (based on the 99th percentile of the loan portfolio's value distribution) has increased by only $7.81 million − $6.97 million = $0.84 million. The reason for this is portfolio diversification. Specifically, built into the joint transition probability matrix in Table 10.1 is a correlation of .3 between the default risks of the two loans.

CreditMetrics: Portfolio VAR Using the Actual Distribution

Unfortunately, the capital requirement under the normal distribution is likely to underestimate the true 99 percent VAR because of the skewness in the actual distribution of loan values. Using Table 10.1 in conjunction with Table 10.3 the 99 percent (worst) loan value for the portfolio is $204.40 million.[11] Thus, the unexpected change in value of the portfolio from its mean value is:

$$\$213.63 \text{ million} - \$204.40 \text{ million} = \$9.23 \text{ million}$$

This is higher than the capital requirement under the normal distribution discussed above ($9.23 million versus $7.81 million), but the benefits of portfolio diversification are clear. In particular,

---

[11] To find this, the probabilities have to be counted backwards: the worst loan outcome, then the next worst, and so on.

the capital requirement of $9.23 million for the combined $200-million face-value portfolio can be favorably compared to the $8.99 million for the single BBB loan of $100 million face value.

CreditMetrics with Large *N* Loans

The normal distribution model can be extended in either of two directions. The first option is to keep expanding the loan joint transition matrix and directly or analytically computing the mean and standard deviation of the portfolio. This, however, rapidly becomes computationally difficult. For example, in a five-loan portfolio, there are 8^5 possible joint transition probabilities, or over 32,000 joint transitions. The second option is to manipulate the equation for the variance of a loan portfolio. It can be shown that the risk of a portfolio of N loans depends on the risk of each pairwise combination of loans in the portfolio as well as the risk of each loan individually. To estimate the risk of a portfolio of N loans, we only need to calculate the risks of subportfolios containing two assets, as shown in the Appendix to this chapter.

For computing the distribution of loan values in the large sample case where loan values are *not* normally distributed, CreditMetrics uses Monte Carlo simulation.

Consider the portfolio of loans in Table 10.4 and the correlations among those loans (borrowers) in Table 10.5.

For each loan, 20,000 (or more) different underlying borrower asset values are simulated, based on the original rating of the loan, the joint transition probabilities to other grades, and the historical correlations among the loans.[12] The loan (or borrower) can either stay in its original rating class or migrate to another rating

---

[12] Technically, decompose the correlation matrix (Σ) among the loans using the Cholesky factorization process, which finds two matrices A and A' (its transpose) such that $\Sigma = AA'$. Asset return scenarios (y) are generated by multiplying the matrix A' (which contains memory relating to historical correlation relationships) by a random number vector z, i.e., $y = A'z$.

Table 10.4   Example Portfolio

Credit Asset	Principal Rating	Maturity Amount	Market (Years)	Value
1	AAA	$ 7,000,000	3	$ 7,821,049
2	AA	1,000,000	4	1,177,268
3	A	1,000,000	3	1,120,831
4	BBB	1,000,000	4	1,189,432
5	BB	1,000,000	3	1,154,641
6	B	1,000,000	4	1,263,523
7	CCC	1,000,000	2	1,127,628
8	A	10,000,000	8	14,229,071
9	BB	5,000,000	2	5,386,603
10	A	3,000,000	2	3,181,246
11	A	1,000,000	4	1,181,246
12	A	2,000,000	5	2,483,322
13	B	600,000	3	705,409
14	B	1,000,000	2	1,087,841
15	B	3,000,000	2	3,263,523
16	B	2,000,000	4	2,527,046
17	BBB	1,000,000	6	1,315,720
18	BBB	8,000,000	5	10,020,611
19	BBB	1,000,000	3	1,118,178
20	AA	5,000,000	5	6,181,784

Source: CREDITMETRICS-Technical Document, April 2, 1997, p. 121.

class. (See the earlier discussion and Figure 10.2.) Each loan is then revalued after each simulation (and rating transition). Adding across the simulated values for the 20 loans produces 20,000 different values for the loan portfolio as a whole. A VAR for the loan portfolio, based on the 99 percent worst case, can be calculated as the value of the loan portfolio that has the 200th worst value out of 20,000 possible loan portfolio values. In

Table 10.5 Asset Correlations for Example Portfolio

	1	2	3	4	5	6	7	8	9	10	11	12	13	14	15	16	17	18	19	20
1	1	0.45	0.45	0.45	0.15	0.15	0.15	0.15	0.15	0.15	0.1	0.1	0.1	0.1	0.1	0.1	0.1	0.1	0.1	0.1
2	0.45	1	0.45	0.45	0.15	0.15	0.15	0.15	0.15	0.15	0.1	0.1	0.1	0.1	0.1	0.1	0.1	0.1	0.1	0.1
3	0.45	0.45	1	0.45	0.15	0.15	0.15	0.15	0.15	0.15	0.1	0.1	0.1	0.1	0.1	0.1	0.1	0.1	0.1	0.1
4	0.45	0.45	0.45	1	0.15	0.15	0.15	0.15	0.15	0.15	0.1	0.1	0.1	0.1	0.1	0.1	0.1	0.1	0.1	0.1
5	0.15	0.15	0.15	0.15	1	0.35	0.35	0.35	0.35	0.35	0.2	0.2	0.2	0.2	0.2	0.15	0.15	0.15	0.1	0.1
6	0.15	0.15	0.15	0.15	0.35	1	0.35	0.35	0.35	0.35	0.2	0.2	0.2	0.2	0.2	0.15	0.15	0.15	0.1	0.1
7	0.15	0.15	0.15	0.15	0.35	0.35	1	0.35	0.35	0.35	0.2	0.2	0.2	0.2	0.2	0.15	0.15	0.15	0.1	0.1
8	0.15	0.15	0.15	0.15	0.35	0.35	0.35	1	0.35	0.35	0.2	0.2	0.2	0.2	0.2	0.15	0.15	0.15	0.1	0.1
9	0.15	0.15	0.15	0.15	0.35	0.35	0.35	0.35	1	0.35	0.2	0.2	0.2	0.2	0.2	0.15	0.15	0.15	0.1	0.1
10	0.15	0.15	0.15	0.15	0.35	0.35	0.35	0.35	0.35	1	0.2	0.2	0.2	0.2	0.2	0.15	0.15	0.15	0.1	0.1
11	0.1	0.1	0.1	0.1	0.2	0.2	0.2	0.2	0.2	0.2	1	0.45	0.45	0.45	0.45	0.2	0.2	0.2	0.1	0.1
12	0.1	0.1	0.1	0.1	0.2	0.2	0.2	0.2	0.2	0.2	0.45	1	0.45	0.45	0.45	0.2	0.2	0.2	0.1	0.1
13	0.1	0.1	0.1	0.1	0.2	0.2	0.2	0.2	0.2	0.2	0.45	0.45	1	0.45	0.45	0.2	0.2	0.2	0.1	0.1
14	0.1	0.1	0.1	0.1	0.2	0.2	0.2	0.2	0.2	0.2	0.45	0.45	0.45	1	0.45	0.2	0.2	0.2	0.1	0.1
15	0.1	0.1	0.1	0.1	0.2	0.2	0.2	0.2	0.2	0.2	0.45	0.45	0.45	0.45	1	0.2	0.2	0.2	0.1	0.1
16	0.1	0.1	0.1	0.1	0.15	0.15	0.15	0.15	0.15	0.15	0.2	0.2	0.2	0.2	0.2	1	0.55	0.55	0.25	0.25
17	0.1	0.1	0.1	0.1	0.15	0.15	0.15	0.15	0.15	0.15	0.2	0.2	0.2	0.2	0.2	0.55	1	0.55	0.25	0.25
18	0.1	0.1	0.1	0.1	0.15	0.15	0.15	0.15	0.15	0.15	0.2	0.2	0.2	0.2	0.2	0.55	0.55	1	0.25	0.25
19	0.1	0.1	0.1	0.1	0.1	0.1	0.1	0.1	0.1	0.1	0.1	0.1	0.1	0.1	0.1	0.25	0.25	0.25	1	0.65
20	0.1	0.1	0.1	0.1	0.1	0.1	0.1	0.1	0.1	0.1	0.1	0.1	0.1	0.1	0.1	0.25	0.25	0.25	0.65	1

Source: CREDITMETRICS-Technical Document, April 2, 1997, p. 122.

conjunction with the mean loan portfolio value, a capital requirement can be calculated.

The CreditMetrics portfolio methodology can also be used for calculating the marginal risk contribution for individual loans. Unlike the KMV-type approach, funds are viewed as being flexibly adjustable to accommodate an expanded loan supply, and "marginal" means loans are either made or not made to a borrower (rather than having an incremental amount of new loans made to a current borrower).

Table 10.6 shows the stand-alone and marginal risk contributions of 20 loans in a hypothetical loan portfolio based on a standard deviation (σ) measure of risk. The stand-alone columns reflect the dollar and percentage risk of each loan, viewed separately. The stand-alone percentage risk for the CCC-rated asset (number 7) is 22.67 percent, and the B-rated asset (number 15) is 18.72 percent. The marginal risk contribution columns in Table 10.5 reflect the risk of adding each loan to a portfolio of the remaining 19 loans (the standard deviation risk of a 20-loan portfolio minus the standard deviation risk of a 19-loan portfolio). Interestingly, in Table 10.6, on a stand-alone basis, asset 7 (CCC) is riskier than asset 15 (B), but when risk is measured in a portfolio context (by its marginal risk contribution), asset 15 is riskier. The reason can be seen from the correlation matrix in Table 10.5, where the B-rated loan (asset 15) has a "high" correlation level of .45 with assets 11, 12, 13, and 14. By comparison, the highest correlations of the CCC-rated loan (asset 7) are with assets 5, 6, 8, 9, and 10 at the .35 level.

One policy implication is immediate and is shown in Figure 10.3, where the total risk (in a portfolio context) of a loan is broken down into two components: (1) its percentage marginal standard deviation (vertical axis) and (2) the dollar amount of credit exposure (horizontal axis). We then have:

Total risk of a loan ($) = Marginal standard deviation (%)
× Credit exposure ($)

Table 10.6 **Standard Deviation of Value Change**

		Stand-Alone		Marginal	
Asset	Credit Rating	Absolute ($)	Percent	Absolute ($)	Percent
1	AAA	4,905	0.06	239	0.00
2	AA	2,007	0.17	114	0.01
3	A	17,523	1.56	693	0.06
4	BBB	40,043	3.37	2,934	0.25
5	BB	99,607	8.63	16,046	1.39
6	B	162,251	12.84	37,664	2.98
7	CCC	255,680	<u>22.67</u>	73,079	<u>6.48</u>
8	A	197,152	1.39	35.104	0.25
9	BB	380,141	7.06	105,949	1.97
10	A	63,207	1.99	5,068	0.16
11	A	15,360	1.30	1,232	0.10
12	A	43,085	1.73	4,531	0.18
13	B	107,314	15.21	25,684	3.64
14	B	167,511	15.40	44,827	4.12
15	B	610,900	<u>18.72</u>	270,000	<u>8.27</u>
16	B	322,720	12.77	89,190	3.53
17	BBB	28,051	2.13	2,775	0.21
18	BBB	306,892	3.06	69,624	0.69
19	BBB	1,837	0.16	120	0.01
20	AA	9,916	0.16	389	0.01

Source: CREDITMETRICS-Technical Document, April 2, 1997, p. 130.

Thus, for the B-rated loan:

$$\$270,000 = 8.27 \text{ percent} \times \$3,263,523$$

Also plotted in Figure 10.3 is an equal risk "isoquant" of $70,000. Suppose managers wish to impose total credit risk exposure limits of $70,000 on each loan measured in a portfolio context. Then asset 15 (the B-rated loan) and assets 16 and 9 are clear

Figure 10.3   Credit Limits and Loan Selection
in the CreditMetrics Framework

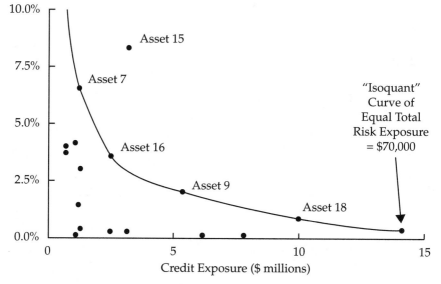

Marginal Standard Deviation

Source: CREDITMETRICS-Technical Document, April 2, 1997, p. 131.

"outliers." One possible solution would be for the bank to sell asset 15 to another bank, or to swap it for another B-rated asset that has a lower correlation with the other loans (assets) in the bank's portfolio. In doing so, its expected returns may remain approximately unchanged, but its loan portfolio risk is likely to decrease.

OTHER PORTFOLIO APPROACHES

CreditPortfolioView and Credit Risk Plus can be viewed as partial MPT models, similar to CreditMetrics, in that the returns on loans and the loan portfolio are not explicitly modeled.

The role of diversification in CreditPortfolioView can best be seen in the context of the macro shock factors (or unsystematic risk factors) U and V (see Chapter 5), which drive the probability of borrower default over time. As portfolio diversification increases— e.g., across countries in the CreditPortfolioView model—the relative importance of unsystematic risk to systematic risk will shrink, and the exposure of a loan portfolio to shocks will shrink. Thus, in the context of the Monte Carlo simulations of the model, the 99 percent worst-case loss for an internationally well-diversified portfolio is likely to be less (other things equal) than that for a one-country or industry-specialized portfolio of loans.

In Credit Risk Plus, we need to distinguish between two model cases. In what was called Model 1 in Chapter 7, there were two sources of uncertainty in the loan portfolio: (1) the Poisson distribution of the number of defaults (around a constant mean default rate) and (2) the severity of losses (variable across loan exposure bands). Because the Poisson distribution implies that each loan has a small probability of default and that this probability is independent across loans, the correlation of default rates is, by definition, zero. In Model 2, however, where the mean default rate itself is variable (gamma distributed), correlations will be induced among the loans in the portfolio because of their varying systematic linkages to the mean default rate movements. As was discussed in Chapter 8, the movement in the mean default rate can be modeled in terms of factor sensitivities to different independent "sectors" (which could be countries or industries). For example, a company's default probability may be sensitive to both a U.S. factor and a German factor. Given this trait, the default correlations in Credit Risk Plus are shown to be equal to:

$$\rho_{AB} = \left(m_A m_B \right)^{\frac{1}{2}} \sum_{k=1}^{N} \theta_{Ak} \theta_{Bk} \left(\frac{\sigma_k}{m_k} \right)^2 \tag{10.17}$$

where ρ_{AB} = default correlation between obligor A and B,

m_A = mean default rate for type A obligor,

m_B = mean default rate for type B obligor,

θ_A = allocation of obligor A's default rate volatility across N sectors,

θ_B = allocation of obligor B's default rate volatility across N sectors,

$(\sigma_k/m_k)^2$ = proportional default rate volatility in sector k.

Table 10.7 shows an example of equation (10.17) where each of the two obligors is sensitive to one economy-wide sector only $(\theta_{Ak} = \theta_{Bk} = 1)$ and $\sigma_k/m_k = .7$ is set at an empirically reasonable level, reflecting national default rate statistics. As can be seen from Table 10.7, as the credit quality of the obligors declines (i.e., m_A and m_B get larger), correlations get larger. Nevertheless, even in the case where individual mean default rates are high ($m_A = 10$ percent and $m_B = 7$ percent), the correlation among the borrowers is still quite small (here, 4.1 percent).

It is also useful to discuss correlations derived from intensity-based models. The correlations among defaults reflect the effect of events in inducing *simultaneous* jumps in the default intensities of obligors. The causes of defaults themselves are not modeled explicitly; however, what are modeled are various approaches to default-arrival intensity that focus on correlated

Table 10.7   The Link between Mean Default Rates and Default Correlations

M_A	0.5%	5%	10%
M_B	1%	2%	7%
θ_{Ak}	1	1	1
θ_{Bk}	1	1	1
σ_k/M_k	70%	70%	70%
ρ_{AB}	0.35%	1.55%	4.1%

Source: Credit Risk+, technical document, Credit Suisse Financial Products, October 1997.

"times to default." This allows the model to answer questions such as: What was the worst week, month, year, etc., out of the past N years, in terms of loan portfolio risk? That worst period will be when correlated default intensities were highest (defaults arrived at the same time). With joint credit events, some of the default intensity of each obligor is tied to such an event with some probability. For example, the intensity-based model of Duffie and Singleton (1998) allows for default intensities to be correlated via both changes in default intensities themselves and joint credit events.[13] These authors discuss various algorithms to estimate default correlation intensities, and provide an excellent review of the intensity-modeling literature.

SUMMARY

This chapter has reviewed various approaches toward applying MPT-type models to the loan portfolio.

Most of the new models are not full-fledged MPT models (returns are often left unmodeled), but their importance is in the link they show between (1) default correlations and loan portfolio risk and (2) portfolio diversification and loan portfolio risk. In particular, the consensus of the literature so far appears to be that default correlations on average are generally low and gains through loan portfolio diversification are potentially high. Moreover, an important implication of these models is that the current 8 percent BIS risk-based capital ratio, which ignores correlations among loans in setting capital requirements, may be

---

[13] One model discussed by Duffie and Singleton (1998) gives a good flavor of the approach. This model is based on correlated jump intensity processes. In this model, obligors have default intensities that mean-revert with correlated Poisson arrivals of randomly sized jumps. They then formulate individual obligor default intensity times as multivariate exponentials, which allows them to develop a model for simulating correlated defaults.

flawed. In particular, MPT-based models suggest that loan portfolios in which individual loan default risks are highly correlated should have higher capital requirements than loan portfolios of the same size, in which default risk correlations are relatively low. By contrast, the BIS regulations specify that the same capital requirement is to be imposed for equally sized portfolios of private-sector loans, no matter what their country, industry or borrower composition.

Appendix **10.1**

The Simplified Two-Asset Subportfolio Solution to the *N* Asset Portfolio Case

The standard formula for the risk of a portfolio is:

$$\sigma_p^2 = \sum_{i=1}^{n} \sigma^2(V_i) + 2 \cdot \sum_{i=1}^{n-1} \sum_{j=i+1}^{n} COV(V_i, V_j) \qquad (10.1A)$$

Alternatively, we may relate the covariance terms to the variances of pairs of assets, where

$$\sigma^2(V_i + V_j) = \sigma^2(V_i) + 2 \cdot COV(V_i, V_j) + \sigma^2(V_j) \qquad (10.2A)$$

and thus

$$2COV(V_i, V_j) = \sigma^2(V_i + V_j) - \sigma^2(V_i) - \sigma^2(V_j) \qquad (10.3A)$$

substituting the equation for $2COV(V_i, V_j)$ in equation (10.1A), we can express the portfolio standard deviation in terms of the standard deviations of subportfolios containing two assets:

$$\sigma_p^2 = \sum_{i=1}^{n-1} \sum_{j=i+1}^{n} \sigma^2(V_i + V_j) - (n-2) \cdot \sum_{i=1}^{n} \sigma^2(V_i) \qquad (10.4A)$$

Chapter *11*

Back-Testing and Stress-Testing Credit Risk Models

INTRODUCTION

A key issue for bankers and regulators is internal model valida-
tion and predictive accuracy. In the context of market models, this
issue has led to numerous efforts to "back-test" models to ascer-
tain their predictive accuracy. Currently, under the BIS market
risk-based capital requirements, a bank must back-test its internal market model over a minimum of 250 past days if it is used for
capital requirement calculations. If the forecast VAR errors on
those 250 days are too large (i.e., risk is underestimated on too
many days), a system of penalties is imposed by regulators to create incentives for bankers to get their models right.[1]

---

[1] Under the internal model rules of the BIS for market risk, the bank's internal
VAR has to be multiplied by a minimum value of 3. Intuitively, this 3 can be
viewed as a stress-test multiplier accommodating outliers in the 99 percent
tail of the distribution. If, in back-testing a model, regulators/auditors find
that the model underestimated VAR on fewer than 4 days out of the past 250
days, it is placed in a green zone and the VAR multiplier remains at its minimum value of 3. If between 4 days and 9 days of underestimated risk is found
(out of 250 days), the model is placed in the yellow zone and the multiplier is
increased to a range from 3.4 to 3.85. If more than 10 daily errors are found,
the multiplication factor for the internal VAR is set at 4 (the model is placed in
the red zone). Some observers have labeled this regulatory punishment system "the traffic-light" system.

Many observers have argued, however, that back-testing over 250 days is simply not enough, given the high standard errors that are likely to be involved if the period is not representative. To show the likelihood of this type of error, the Appendix to this chapter runs through a simple foreign exchange (FX) example of back-testing a market VAR model based on historical simulation. To reduce error of this type, one suggestion has been to increase the number of past daily observations over which a back-test of a model is conducted. For example, at least 1,000 past daily observations are commonly felt to be adequate to ensure that the period chosen is "representative" in terms of testing the predictive accuracy of any given model. Unfortunately, even for traded financial assets such as currencies, a period of 1,000 past days requires going back in time over 4 years and may involve covering a wide and unrepresentative range of FX regimes.

BACK-TESTING CREDIT RISK MODELS

To appropriately back-test or stress-test market-risk models, 250 observations may be regarded as too few, but it is unlikely that a bank would be able to generate anywhere near that many past time-series observations for back-testing its internal credit-risk models. For example, with annual observations (which are the most likely to be available), a bank might be able to generate only 40 past observations that cover 5 or 6 credit cycles.[2] A banker/regulator is then severely hampered from performing time-series back-testing similar to that currently available for market risk models.

---

[2] Even this is somewhat optimistic; not even the rating agencies have default histories going back that far. Currently, most banks have perhaps two or three years' usable data.

Time-Series vs. Cross-Sectional Stress Testing

In a recent set of a papers, Granger and Huang (1997), at a theoretical level, and Carey (1998) and Lopez and Saidenberg (1998), at a simulation/empirical level, show that stress tests similar to those conducted across time for market risk models, can be conducted using cross-sectional or panel data for credit risk models. In particular, suppose in any given year a bank has a sample of N loans in its portfolio, where N is large. By repeated subsampling of the total loan portfolio, it is possible to build up a cross-sectional distribution of expected losses, unexpected losses, and the full probability density function of losses. By comparing cross-sectional subportfolio loss distributions with the actual full-portfolio loss distribution, it is possible to generate an idea of the predictive accuracy of a credit risk model. For example, if the model is a good predictor or forecaster, the mean average loss rate and the mean 99th percentile loss rate from 10,000 randomly drawn subportfolios of the total loan portfolio should be pretty close to the actual average and 99th percentile loss rates on the full loan portfolio experienced in that year. Indeed, different models may have different prediction errors, and the relative size of the prediction errors can be used to judge the "best" model [see Lopez and Saidenberg (1998)].

A number of statistical issues arise with cross-sectional stress testing, but these are generally similar to those that arise with time-series stress testing (or back-testing). The first issue is that the number of loans in the portfolio has to be large. For example, Carey's (1998) sample is based on 30,000 privately placed bonds held by a dozen life insurance companies during 1986 to 1992, a period during which over 300 credit-related events (defaults, debt restructurings, and so on) occurred for the issuers of the bonds. The subsamples chosen varied in size; for example, portfolios of $.5 billion to $15 billion in size containing no more than 3 percent of the bonds of any one issuer. Table 11.1 shows simulated loss rates from 50,000 subsample portfolios drawn from the 30,000-bond population. Subportfolios were limited to $1 billion in size.

Table 11.1   Loss Rate Distribution When Monte Carlo Draws Are from Good versus Bad Years

This table compares Monte Carlo estimates of portfolio loss rates at the mean and at various percentiles of the credit loss rate distribution, when Monte Carlo draws are limited to the "good" years, 1986–1989, the "bad" years, 1990–1992, and the "worst" year, 1991. All drawn portfolios are $1 billion in size. The two panels, each with three rows, report results when all simulated portfolio assets are investment grade and below investment grade (rated <BBB), respectively. An exposure-to-one-borrower limit of 3 percent of the portfolio size was enforced in building simulated portfolios. Results in each row are based on 50,000 simulated portfolios.

Portfolio Characteristics		Simulated Portfolio Loss Rates (Percent)						
% Rated <BBB	Years Used in Monte Carlo	Mean	At Loss Distribution Percentiles					
			95	97.5	99	99.5	99.9	99.95
0%	Good: 1986–1989	0.09	0.53	0.74	1.40	1.46	1.98	2.14
0%	Bad: 1990–1992	0.15	0.87	1.26	1.45	1.59	2.22	2.28
0%	Very Bad: 1991	0.16	0.91	1.40	1.54	1.67	2.28	2.36
100%	Good: 1986–1989	1.73	4.18	4.63	5.11	5.43	5.91	6.05
100%	Bad: 1990–1992	2.53	5.59	6.31	7.19	7.82	8.95	9.33
100%	Very Bad: 1991	3.76	6.68	7.30	8.04	8.55	9.72	10.19

Source: Mark Carey, "Credit Risk in Private Debt Portfolios," *Journal of Finance,* Vol. 53, August, 1998, pp. 1363–1387.

The loss rates vary by year. In 1991, which was the trough of the last U.S. recession, 50,000 simulated portfolios containing below-investment-grade (< BBB) bonds, produced a (mean) 99 percent loss rate of 8.04 percent, which is quite close to the BIS 8 percent risk-based capital requirement. However, notice that in relatively good years (e.g., 1986–1989), the 99 percent loss rate was much lower: 5.11 percent.

The second issue is the effect of outliers on simulated loss distributions. A few extreme outliers can seriously affect the mean, variance, skew and kurtosis of an estimated distribution, as well as the correlations among the loans implied in the portfolio. In a market risk model context, Stahl (1998) has shown how only 5 outliers out of 1,000, in terms of foreign currency exchange rates, can have a major impact on estimated correlations among key currencies. With respect to credit risk, the danger is that a few big defaults in any given year could seriously bias the predictive power of any cross-sectional test of a given model.

The third issue, and perhaps the most worrisome, is the representativeness of any given year or subperiod chosen to evaluate statistical moments such as the mean (expected) loss rate and the 99 percent unexpected loss rate. Suppose we look at 1991, a recession year. A set of systematic and unsystematic risk factors likely determined the intensity of the recession. The more a recession year reflects systematic rather than unsystematic recession risk factors, the more representative the loss experience of that year is, in "a predictive" sense, for future bad recession years. This suggests that some type of screening tests need to be conducted on various recession years before a given year's loss experience is chosen as a benchmark for testing predictive accuracy among credit risk models and for calculating capital requirements.[3]

---

[3] The analogy with back-testing market risk models using time-series data is linked to how representative the past period is (i.e., the last 250 days under the BIS rules).

SUMMARY

A key measure of the usefulness of internal credit risk models is their predictive ability. Tests of predictive ability—such as back-testing—are difficult for credit risk models because of the lack of sufficiently long time-series data. Nevertheless, given a large and representative (in a default risk sense) loan portfolio, it is possible to stress-test credit risk models by using cross-sectional subport-folio sampling techniques that provide predictive information on average loss rates and unexpected loss rates. Moreover, the predictive accuracy—in a cross-sectional sense—of different models can be used to choose among different models. In the future, wider-panel data sets, and even time-series of loan loss experience, are likely to be developed by banks and/or consortia of banks. Because we are at the beginning of such an exercise, it is important to note that, to be really useful, these loan portfolio experience data sets should include not only loss experience but also the conditioning variables that the different models require (e.g., recoveries, loan size, ratings, interest rates, fees, and so on; see Chapter 8).

VAR and Market Risk Models: The Historic Simulation Approach

The essential idea is to take a market portfolio of assets (FX, bonds, equities, and so on) and revalue them based on the actual prices (returns) that existed on these assets the day before, the day before that, and so on. For example, an FI might calculate the VAR of its FX portfolio based on prices (exchange rates) that existed for these assets on each of the prior 500 days.

Consider the example in Table 11.1A, where a U.S. FI is trading two currencies: the Japanese yen and the Swiss franc. At the close of trade on December 1, 2000, it has a long position in Japanese yen of 500,000,000 ¥ and a long position in Swiss francs of 20,000,000 SF. It wants to assess its 5 percent VAR; that is, if tomorrow is that one bad day in 20 (the 5 percent bad-day case), how much does it stand to lose on its total foreign currency position? As shown in Table 11.1A, six steps are required to calculate the VAR of its currency portfolio. The same methodological approach would be followed to calculate the VAR of any asset or liability (e.g., bonds, loans, and so on), as long as market prices are available over a sufficiently long time period.

Step 1. Measure Exposures

Convert today's foreign currency positions into dollar equivalents, using today's exchange rates. Thus, evaluating its FX position

Table 11.1A   Hypothetical Example of the Historic or Back-Simulation VAR Approach Using Two Currencies as of December 1, 2000

Step 1. Measure Exposures	Yen (¥)	Swiss Francs (SF)
1. Closing position on December 1, 2000	500,000,000	20,000,000
2. Exchange rate on December 1, 2000	¥130/$1	SF 1.4/$1
3. US$ Equivalent position on December 1, 2000	$3,846,154	$14,285,714
Step 2. Measure Sensitivity		
4. 1.01 × Current exchange rate	¥131.3	SF 1.414
5. Revalued position ($)	$3,808,073	$14,144,272
6. Delta of position ($) (Measure of sensitivity to a 1 percent adverse change in exchange rate, or item 5 minus item 3)	−$38,081	−$141,442

Step 3. Measure Risk on December 1, 2000, Closing Position, Using Exchange Rates That Existed on Each of the Last 500 Days

November 30, 2000

	Yen (¥)	Swiss Francs (SF)
7. Change in exchange rate (%) on November 30, 2000	0.5%	0.2%
8. Risk (delta × change in exchange rate)	−$19,040.5	−$28,288.4
9. Sum of risks = −$47,328.9		

Step 4. Repeat Step 3 for Each of the Remaining 499 Days

November 29, 2000	. . .	. . .
April 15, 1999	. . .	. . .
November 30, 1998	. . .	. . .

(continued)

Table 11.1A   (Continued)

Step 5. Rank Days by Risk, from Worst to Best

Day	Date	Risk ($)
1	May 6, 1999	−105,669
2	January 27, 2000	−103,276
3	December 1, 1998	−90,939
⋮		
25	November 30, 2000	−47,328.9
⋮		
499	April 8, 2000	+98,833
500	July 28, 1999	+108,376

Step 6. VAR (25th Worst Day Out of Last 500)

VAR = $47,328.9 (November 30, 2000)

This is the predicted VAR on the next trading day (December 2, 2000, in our example).

on December 1, 2000, the FI has a long position of $3,846,154 in yen and $14,285,714 in Swiss francs.

STEP 2. MEASURE SENSITIVITY

Measure the sensitivity of each FX position by calculating its delta, where delta measures the change in the dollar value of each FX position if the yen and Swiss franc depreciate (decline in value) by 1 percent against the dollar. As can be seen from line 6 of Table 11.1A, the delta is −$38,081 for the Japanese yen position and −$141,442 for the Swiss franc position.

STEP 3. MEASURE RISK

Look at the actual percentages of changes in exchange rates (¥/$ and SF/$) on each of the past 500 days. Thus, during the day of November 30, 2000, the yen declined in value against the dollar by

0.5 percent, and the Swiss franc declined in value against the dollar by 0.2 percent. (If the currencies were to appreciate in value against the dollar, the sign against the number in line 7 of Table 11.1A would be negative, because fewer units of foreign currency are needed to buy a dollar than were needed the day before.) In line 8, combining the delta (for a 1% change) and the actual percentage change in each FX rate means a total loss of $47,328.9 if the FI had held the current ¥500,000,000 and SF 20,000,000 positions on November 30, 2000.

STEP 4. REPEAT STEP 3

Step 4 repeats the same exercise for the yen and Swiss franc positions, but uses the actual exchange rate changes on November 29, 2000, November 28, 2000, and so on. The FX losses/gains on each of the past 500 trading days are calculated, excluding weekends and holidays on which the FX market is closed. This amounts to going back in time over 2 years. For each of these days, the actual change in exchange rates is calculated (line 7) and multiplied by the delta of each position (the numbers in line 6 of Table 11.1A). These two numbers are summed to attain total risk measures for each of the past 500 days.

STEP 5. RANK DAYS BY RISK, FROM WORST TO BEST

These risk measures can then be ranked from worst to best. The worst-case loss would have occurred on this position on May 6, 1999, when the total loss was $105,669. This "worst-case scenario" would be of interest to FI managers, but we are interested, in this example, in the 5 percent worst case; that is, a loss exceeding this size doesn't occur more than 25 days out of the 500 days (25/500 equals 5 percent). In our example, the 25th worst loss out of 500 occurred on November 30, 2000. The loss amounted to $47,328.9.

Step 6. VAR

If it is assumed that the recent past distribution of exchange rates is an accurate predictor of the likely distribution of FX rate changes in the near future—that is, that exchange rate changes have a "stationary" distribution—then the $47,328.9 can be viewed as the FX VAR exposure of the FI on December 1, 2000. If the next day (in our case, December 2, 2000) is a bad day in the FX markets, and given the FI's position of long ¥500 million and long SF 20 million, the FI can expect to lose $47,328.9 (or more) with a 5 percent probability. This VAR prediction can then be compared with the actual loss/gain realization on December 2, 2000. The VAR measure is then updated every day as the FX position changes, as does the delta and the components of the 500-day window, with one day dropped (the oldest) and one day added (the most recent). For example, given the nature of FX trading, the positions held on December 5, 2000, could be very different from those held on December 1, 2000. Further, one major exchange rate change between December 1 and 5 could have a major impact on the 5 percent VAR calculated during moving 500-day window periods. The predicted (next day's) VAR is compared with the actual FX gains/losses realized on that day for each of the following 250 days (assuming 250 trading days from December 2, 2000, to December 1, 2001). We also assume that the back-testing is being done on December 2, 2001, and the regulator/model auditor is evaluating the model's performance over the prior 250 days (December 2, 2000, to December 1, 2001). If the model is "predictively" correct, realized losses should equal or exceed the model VARs on 12½ days of the 250 trading days (5 percent of the time). If the realized losses exceed the model VARs on more than 12½ days, either there is model error or the 250-day span is too short or unrepresentative to test the model's validity. For example, the 500-day window may be too narrow to historically simulate VARs, and/or 250 days may be an "unrepresentative" period to stress-test the model.

Chapter **12**

RAROC Models

INTRODUCTION

Today, virtually all major banks and FIs have developed RAROC (risk-adjusted return on capital) models to evaluate the profitability of various business lines, including their lending. The RAROC concept was first introduced by Bankers Trust in the 1970s. The recent surge among banks and other FIs to adopt proprietary forms of the RAROC approach can be explained by two major forces: (1) the demand by stockholders for improved performance, especially the maximization of shareholder value, and (2) the growth of FI conglomerates built around separate business units (or profit centers). These two developments have been the impetus for banks to develop a measure of performance that is comparable across business units, especially when the capital of the bank is both costly and limited.

WHAT IS RAROC?

In terms of modern portfolio theory (MPT), RAROC can best be thought of as a Sharpe ratio for business units, including lending. Its numerator, as explained below, is some measure of adjusted income over either a future period (the next year) or a past period (last year). The denominator is a measure of the unexpected loss or economic capital at risk (VAR) as a result of that activity. Thus:

$$\text{RAROC} = \frac{\text{Adjusted income}}{\text{Capital at risk}} \qquad (12.1)$$

In this chapter, we will concentrate on the measurement of RAROC in terms of lending, although, as noted above, it can be applied across all areas of the bank.[1] Once calculated, the RAROC of a loan is meant to be compared with some hurdle rate reflecting the bank's cost of funds or the opportunity cost of stockholders in holding equity in the bank. Thus, in some RAROC models, the hurdle rate is the bank stockholders' return on equity (ROE); in others, it is some measure of the weighted-average cost of capital (WACC).[2]

If:

$$\text{RAROC} > \text{Hurdle rate} \qquad (12.2)$$

then the loan is viewed as value-adding, and scarce bank capital should be allocated to the activity.

Because RAROC historically has been calculated on a stand-alone basis, with correlations among activities ignored, the number of projects/activities satisfying equation (12.2) often exceeds the available (economic) capital of the bank. It may take time to raise new equity to fund all "valuable" projects (in a RAROC sense), so a second-round allocation of economic capital usually takes place [see Dermine (1998) and Crouhy, Turnbull, and Wakeman (1998)]. This is to calculate a weight (w_j) such that:

$$w_j = EC_B \big/ \sum_{j=1}^{n} EC_j \qquad (12.3)$$

---

[1] According to Zaik, Walter, and Kelling (1996), Bank of America applies its RAROC model to 46 different business units within the bank.

[2] In general, WACC will be less than ROE, especially if debt costs are tax-deductible.

where EC_B is the available economic capital of the bank and EC_j is the stand-alone economic capital allocation to the viable (acceptable) projects under equation (12.2). Marginal economic capital allocated for the jth business unit is:

$$w_j EC_j \qquad (12.4)$$

and across all business units:

$$\sum_{j=1}^{n} w_j EC_j = EC_B \qquad (12.5)$$

RAROC vs. ROA vs. RORAC

Before looking at the different forms that RAROC can take, it is worthwhile to briefly compare RAROC with ROA (return on assets) and RORAC (return on risk-adjusted capital). The formulas for these alternative (loan) performance measures are:

$$\text{ROA} = \frac{\text{Adjusted income}}{\text{Assets lent}} \qquad (12.6)$$

$$\text{RORAC} = \frac{\text{Adjusted income}}{\text{BIS risk-based capital requirement}} \qquad (12.7)$$

All three measures—RAROC, ROA, and RORAC—potentially calculate income in a similar fashion, but they differ in the calculation of the denominator. Thus, ROA, a traditional measure of performance, completely ignores the risk of the activity of lending, and uses assets lent as the denominator. RORAC uses the BIS regulatory capital requirement as a measure of the capital at risk from the activity. For private-sector loans, this means taking the book value of the outstanding loan and multiplying it by 8 percent. By comparison, the alternative forms of RAROC discussed below seek to more accurately measure the economic or VAR exposure from lending activity.

Alternative Forms of RAROC

We will discuss here the two components of the ratio: (1) the numerator and (2) the denominator.

The Numerator

As shown in equation (12.1), the numerator reflects the adjusted expected one-year income on a loan. The numerator can reflect all or a subset of the factors in equation (12.8):

$$\text{Adjusted income} = \text{Spread} + \text{Fees} - (\text{Expected loss}) - (\text{Operating costs}) \quad (12.8)$$

The spread term reflects the direct income earned on the loan—essentially, the difference between the loan rate and the bank's cost of funds. To this should be added fees directly attributable to the loan over the next year. For example, loan origination fees would be added, as would commitment fees. There are, however, a number of "gray" areas. Suppose, in making a loan to a small business, the small business brings its asset management business to the bank (the customer relationship effect) and that business also generates annual fees. A lending officer may view these asset management fees as part of the loan's profitability, and thus the loan's RAROC calculation. The bank's asset manager will also claim some of the fees, as part of his or her RAROC calculation for the asset management unit. The danger is that fees will be double- or triple-counted. A very careful allocation of fees via some allocation matrix is needed, so as to avoid the "double-counting" problem.[3]

---

[3] Nevertheless, some banks take a "customer's relationship" approach and calculate the RAROC for the whole relationship.

In many RAROC models, two deductions are commonly made, from the spread and fees, to calculate adjusted income. The first recognizes that expected losses are part of normal banking business and deducts these from direct income. One way to do this would be to use a KMV-type model where:

$$\text{Expected loss}_i = \text{EDF}_i \times \text{LGD}_i \qquad (12.9)$$

Alternatively, some annual accounting-based loss reserves can be allocated to the loan. As Dermine (1998) notes, this can bias the calculation if there is a link between the loan's maturity and the size of annual loss reserves. Finally, some RAROC models deduct measures of a loan's operating costs, such as a loan officer's time and resources in originating and monitoring the loan. In practice, precise allocation of such costs across loans has proved to be very difficult.

The Denominator

Historically, two approaches have emerged to measure the denominator of the RAROC equation or economic capital at risk. The first approach, following Bankers Trust, develops a market-based measure. The second, following Bank of America among others, develops an experiential or historically based measure.

The original Bankers Trust approach was to measure capital at risk as being equal to the maximum (adverse) change in the market value of a loan over the next year. Starting with the duration equation:

$$\frac{\Delta L}{L} = -D_L \frac{\Delta R}{1 + R_L} \qquad (12.10)$$

($\Delta L/L$) is the percentage change in the market value of the loan expected over the next year, D_L is the Macauley duration of the loan, and ($\Delta R/1 + R_L$) is the expected maximum discounted change in the credit-risk premium on the loan during the next year.[4]

We can rewrite the duration equation with the following interpretation:

ΔL	$=$	$-D_L$	$\times$	L	$\times$	$(\Delta R / 1 + R_L)$	
(Dollar capital risk exposure or loss amount)		(Duration of the loan)		(Risk amount or loan exposure)		(Expected discounted change in the credit premium or risk factor on the loan)	(12.11)

The loan's duration (say, 2.7 years) and the loan amount (say, $1 million) are easily estimated. It is more difficult to estimate the maximum change in the credit risk premium on the loan expected over the next year. Publicly available data on loan risk premiums are scarce, so users of this approach turn to publicly available corporate bond market data to estimate credit risk premiums. First, a Standard and Poor's (S&P) or other rating agencies credit rating (AAA, AA, A, and so on) is assigned to a borrower. Thereafter, the risk premium changes of all the bonds traded in that particular rating class over the past year are analyzed. The ΔR in the RAROC equation is then:

$$\Delta R = \text{Max} \, [\Delta(R_i - R_G) > 0] \tag{12.12}$$

where $\Delta \, (R_i - R_G)$ is the change in the yield spread between corporate bonds of credit rating class i (R_i) and matched-duration Treasury bonds (R_G) over the past year. To consider only the

---

[4] Credit risk is distinguished from market risk in that the interest rate on the loan can be decomposed into:

$$R_L = R_F + R,$$

where R_L is the loan rate, R_F is the credit-risk free (Treasury rate) on a similar duration bond, and R is the credit spread. Here, we are not concerned with changes in R_F (ΔR_F) that affect the loan's market value, but rather with the effects of shifts in R (ΔR), the credit spread.

worst-case scenario, the maximum change in yield spread is chosen, as opposed to the average change.

As an example, let us evaluate the credit risk of a loan to an AAA borrower. Assume there are currently 400 publicly traded bonds in that class (the bonds were issued by firms whose rating type is similar to that of the borrower). The first step is to evaluate the actual changes in the credit risk premiums $(R_i - R_G)$ on each bond for the past year. These (hypothetical) changes are plotted in the frequency curve of Figure 12.1. They range from a fall in the risk premium of 1 percent to an increase of 3.5 percent. Because the largest increase may be a very extreme (unrepresentative) number, the 99 percent worst-case scenario is chosen. (Only 4 bonds out of 400 have risk premium increases exceeding the 99 percent worst case. For the example shown in Figure 12.1, this is equal to 1.1 percent.)

Figure 12.1   Estimating the Change in the Risk Premium

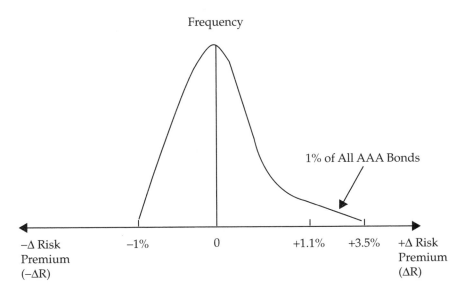

The estimate of loan (or capital) risk, assuming that the current average level of rates on AAA bonds is 10 percent, is:

$$\Delta L = -D_L \times L \times \frac{\Delta R}{1 + R_L}$$

$$= -(2.7)(\$1 \text{ million})\left(\frac{.011}{1.1}\right) \qquad (12.13)$$

$$= -\$27,000$$

Thus, although the face value of the loan amount is $1 million, the risk amount, or change in the loan's market value due to a decline in its credit quality, is $27,000.

To determine whether the loan is worth making, the estimated loan risk is compared to the loan's adjusted income. Suppose the annual projected adjusted income is:[5]

$$\text{Spread} = 0.2 \text{ percent} \times \$1 \text{ million} = \$2,000$$
$$\text{Fees} = 0.15 \text{ percent} \times \$1 \text{ million} = \$1,500$$
$$\text{Expected loss} = 0.1 \text{ percent} \times \$.5 \text{ million} = \underline{\$\ (500)} \quad (12.14)$$
$$\$3,000$$

$$\text{RAROC} = \frac{\text{One-year adjusted income on loan}}{\text{Capital at risk}(\Delta L)} = \frac{\$3,000}{\$27,000}$$

$$= 11.1 \text{ percent}$$

If this RAROC (11.1 percent) exceeds the bank's hurdle rate, the loan should be made.[6] Most banks, however, have adopted a different way to calculate the denominator of the RAROC equation

---

[5] For simplicity, we ignore operating costs here.

[6] Suppose the bank's hurdle was its ROE of 10 percent. Then the loan would be profitable and should be made under the RAROC criterion.

or capital at risk (unexpected loss). The calculation usually involves experiential modeling based on a historic database of loan (or bond) defaults. Essentially, for each type of borrower, the adjusted one-year income is divided by an unexpected default rate, and the result is multiplied by the loss given default (LGD), where the unexpected default rate is some multiple of the historic standard deviation of default rates for such borrowers. The multiple of σ used will reflect both the desired credit rating of the bank and the actual distribution of losses. For example, suppose the bank wants to achieve an AA rating and, on average, only 0.03 percent of AA "firms" default in a year. Consequently, the amount of capital needed has to cover up to 99.97 percent of loan (asset) losses. Based on the standardized normal distribution, the standard deviation of losses (σ) would have to be multiplied by 3.4; that is:[7]

$$\text{Unexpected loss}_i = 3.4 \times \sigma_i \times \text{LGD}_i \times \text{Exposure}_i \quad (12.15)$$

However, as discussed in Chapters 3 through 7, loan loss distributions tend to be skewed and to have "fat tails," and, depending on the fatness of the tail, the multiplier of σ is increased. For example, Zaik, Walter, and Kelling (1996) reported that Bank of America uses a multiplier of 6:

$$\text{Unexpected loss}_i = 6 \times \sigma_i \times \text{LGD}_i \times \text{Exposure} \quad (12.16)$$

Others have argued for a multiplier as high as 10 if a bank wants to achieve AAA status.

---

[7] As discussed earlier, one simple way to calculate σ is to use the binomial model. Based on N years of data, where p_i is the default rate in year i for this borrower type:

$$\sigma = \sqrt{\frac{\sum_{i=1}^{N}(p_i)(1-p_i)}{N}}$$

THE RAROC DENOMINATOR AND CORRELATIONS

Neither the market-based version [equation (12.10)] nor the experientially based version [equation (12.15)] of the RAROC denominator allows for correlations (and thus diversification) among business line risks, including lending. That the RAROC equation should take such correlations into account can be seen by calculating the RAROC from a one-factor capital asset pricing model (CAPM) that describes the equilibrium risk–return trade-offs among assets. This theoretical RAROC includes an adjustment for correlation in its denominator. Specifically, following James (1996) and Crouhy, Turnbull, and Wakeman (1998), the CAPM requires:

$$R_i - R_f = \beta_i (R_m - R_f) \tag{12.17}$$

where R_i = return on a risky asset,
$\quad R_f$ = risk-free rate,
$\quad R_m$ = return on the market portfolio,
$\quad \beta_i$ = systematic risk of the risky asset,

and

$$\beta_i = \frac{\sigma_{im}}{\sigma^2_m} = \frac{\rho_{im}\sigma_i\sigma_m}{\sigma^2_m} = \frac{\rho_{im}\sigma_i}{\sigma_m} \tag{12.18}$$

where $\quad \sigma_{im}$ = covariance between the returns on risky asset i and the market portfolio m,
$\quad \sigma_m$ = standard deviation of the return on the market portfolio,
$\quad \rho_{im}$ = correlation between the returns on the risky asset i and the market portfolio,
$\rho_{im}\sigma_i\sigma_m = \sigma_{im}$, by definition.

Substituting equation (12.18) into equation (12.17), we have:

$$R_i - R_f = \rho_{im}\sigma_i \frac{(R_m - R_f)}{\sigma_m} \tag{12.19}$$

and, rearranging:

$$\frac{R_i - R_f}{\rho_{im} \cdot \sigma_i} = \frac{R_m - R_f}{\sigma_m}$$

$$(\text{RAROC}) = (\text{Hurdle rate}) \qquad (12.20)$$

The left-hand side of equation (12.20) is the theoretical RAROC; the right-hand side is the hurdle rate. As can be seen by setting $\rho_{im} = 1$, the theoretical RAROC takes the stand-alone form employed by most banks, which is the traditional Sharpe ratio $(R_i - R_f / \sigma_i)$ for a risky asset. This will clearly bias against projects for which (excess) returns $(R_i - R_f)$ may be low but which have low correlations with other projects within the bank. Reportedly, some banks are building correlations into their RAROC denominators; that is, they are measuring unexpected loss as:

$$\text{Unexpected loss}_i = \rho_{im} \times \text{Multiplier} \\ \times \sigma_i \times \text{LGD}_i \times \text{Exposure}_i \qquad (12.21)$$

In doing so, two issues arise. First, looking at the correlation of the loan's return with the market (even if estimable) may be erroneous unless the bank is holding a very well diversified portfolio of assets (i.e., the market portfolio). Some multifactor specification of equation (12.17) may be more appropriate in many cases. Second, the RAROC formula in (12.21) becomes nonimplementable if ρ_{im} lies in the range $-1 \leq \rho_{im} \leq 0$.

RAROC AND EVA

There is also a link between RAROC and economic value added (EVA), which is a risk-adjusted performance measure increasingly used by banks and other corporations. In the context of lending, EVA requires a loan to be made only if it adds to the economic value of the bank from the shareholders' perspective. In fact, an EVA formula can be directly developed from the RAROC formula.

Assume ROE is the hurdle rate for RAROC. A loan should be made if:

$$\text{RAROC} > \text{ROE} \tag{12.22}$$

or

$$\frac{\left(\begin{array}{c}\text{Spread} + \text{Fees} - \text{Expected} \\ \text{loss} - \text{Operating costs}\end{array}\right)}{\begin{array}{c}\text{Capital at risk or} \\ \text{economic capital (K)}\end{array}} > \text{ROE} \tag{12.23}$$

Rearranging, the EVA per dollar of the loan is positive if:

$$(\text{Spread} + \text{Fees} - \text{Expected loss} - \text{Operating costs}) - \text{ROE.K} \geq 0$$

Summary

This chapter has discussed the RAROC model of lending (and other business-unit performance). RAROC is similar to a Sharpe ratio commonly analyzed in assessing the performance of risky assets and portfolios of risky assets (such as mutual funds). There are two different approaches to calculating RAROC: (1) the market-based approach and (2) the experiential approach. A major weakness of the RAROC model is its explicit failure to account for correlations. Such an accounting is needed; otherwise, investment decisions will tend to be biased against low-return activities that have high potential diversification value. A direct link between RAROC and EVA was also described.

Chapter **13**

Off-Balance-Sheet Credit Risk

INTRODUCTION

The tremendous growth in off-balance-sheet (OBS) over-the-counter (OTC) contracts, such as swaps, forwards, and customized options, has raised questions as to where credit risk exposure really lies: Is it on or off the balance sheet? For example, at the end of 1997, the total (on-balance-sheet) assets for U.S. banks were $4.9 trillion. The total notional value of their OBS positions was $28.4 trillion, and the notional value of all outstanding interest-rate swaps alone was $8.9 trillion.

Given the growth and importance of OBS exposures, a question arises as to the applicability of the models discussed in Chapters 3 to 12 to OBS activities. To the extent that a model is seeking to predict the probability of default (such as KMV), it is as applicable to the measurement of counterparty default risk on a swap contract as it is to a borrower's defaulting on a loan contract.[1] Where differences arise, however, is in measuring the VAR of an OBS position and assessing the credit risk of a portfolio of OBS positions.

---

[1] Arguably, net short-term obligations (payments) on swap and other OBS contracts have to be added to short-term liabilities on the balance sheet when defining the default exercise point (see Chapter 3).

In this chapter, we will evaluate the credit VAR of OBS contracts. Because of the importance of interest-rate swaps in most banks' OBS portfolios, much of the discussion will be built around these instruments.

MEASURING THE CREDIT RISK AND VAR OF INTEREST RATE SWAPS

As is well known, the credit risk on an interest rate swap is less than the credit risk on an equivalent-size loan [see, for example, Smith, Smithson, and Wilford (1990)]. Specifically, apart from the fact that interest rate swap exposure reflects only the difference between two interest-rate-linked cash flows, rather than the full principal amount as in the case of a loan, at least two conditions have to pertain for a counterparty to default on a swap: (1) the swap contract has to be out-of-the-money to a counterparty (i.e., it has to have an NPV < 0), and (2) the counterparty has to be in financial distress. In addition to these preconditions, banks and other FIs that engage in swaps have put in place a number of other mechanisms that further reduce the probability of default on a swap contract or the loss given default. These mechanisms are:

1. Rationing or capping the notional value of swap exposure to any given counterparty.
2. Establishing bilateral and multilateral netting across contracts (see below).
3. Establishing collateral guarantee requirements.
4. Marking to market long-term swap contracts at relatively frequent intervals.
5. Restricting maturities of contracts.
6. Establishing special-purpose vehicles (with high capitalization) through which to engage in swap contracts.

7. Adjusting the fixed rate of the swap contract for a risk premium that reflects the credit risk of the counterparty.[2]

Building all of these features into a credit VAR model is difficult but not infeasible. Here, we look first at how the BIS calculates the capital requirement for swaps and other OTC derivative instruments, and then at how CreditMetrics and others approach estimating the credit VAR for a plain-vanilla interest-rate swap contract.

CREDIT RISK FOR SWAPS: THE BIS MODEL

Under the BIS risk-based capital ratio rules, a major distinction is made between exchange-traded derivative security contracts (e.g., Chicago Board of Trade exchange-traded options) and over-the-counter (OTC) traded instruments (e.g., forwards, swaps, caps, and floors). The credit or default risk of exchange-traded derivatives is approximately zero because when a counterparty defaults on its obligations, the exchange itself adopts the counterparty's obligations in full. However, no such guarantee exists for bilaterally negotiated OTC contracts originated and traded outside organized exchanges. Hence, most OBS futures and options positions have no capital requirements for a bank, although most forwards, swaps, caps, and floors do.

For the purposes of capital regulation under the BIS codes the calculation of the risk-adjusted asset values of OBS market contracts requires a two-step approach: (1) credit equivalent amounts are calculated for each contract, and (2) the credit equivalent amounts are multiplied by an appropriate risk weight.

Specifically, the notional or face values of all nonexchange-traded swap, forward, and other derivative contracts are first

---

[2] Evidence by Fehle (1998) and Duffie and Huang (1996) suggests that a default risk premium of between ½ bp and 1 bp exists in the spread between the fixed swap rate and a similar maturity Treasury bond in the United States.

converted into credit equivalent amounts. The credit equivalent amount itself is divided into a *potential exposure* element and a *current exposure* element:

$$
\begin{array}{l}
\text{Credit equivalent amount} \\
\text{of OBS derivative} \\
\text{security items (\$)}
\end{array}
=
\begin{array}{l}
\text{Potential exposure (\$)} \\
\text{+Current exposure (\$)}
\end{array}
\quad (13.1)
$$

The potential exposure component reflects the credit risk if the counterparty to the contract defaults in the *future*. The probability of such an occurrence is modeled as depending on the future volatility of interest rates/exchange rates. Based on a Federal Reserve Bank of England Monte Carlo simulation exercise (see Appendix 13.1), the BIS came up with a set of conversion factors that varied by type of contract (e.g., interest rate or FX) and by maturity bucket (see Table 13.1). The potential exposure conversion factors in Table 13.1 are larger for foreign exchange contracts than for interest rate contracts. Also, note the larger potential exposure credit risk for longer-term contracts of both types.

In addition to calculating the potential exposure of an OBS market instrument, a bank must calculate its current exposure to the instrument: the cost of replacing a contract if a counterparty defaults today. The bank calculates this replacement cost

Table 13.1   Credit Conversion Factors for Interest Rate and Foreign Exchange Contracts in Calculating Potential Exposure (as a % of Nominal Contract Value)

Remaining Maturity	(1) Interest Rate Contracts	(2) Exchange Rate Contracts
1. One year or less	0	1.0%
2. One to five years	0.5%	5.0%
3. Over five years	1.5%	7.5%

Source: Federal Reserve Board of Governors press release, August 1995, Section II.

or current exposure by replacing the rate or price that was initially in the contract with the current rate or price for a similar contract, and then recalculates all the current and future cash flows to give a current present-value measure of the replacement cost of the contract.

If NPV > 0, then the replacement value equals current exposure. However, if NPV < 0, then current exposure is set to zero because a bank cannot be allowed to gain by defaulting on an out-of-the money contract.

After the current and potential exposure amounts are summed to produce the credit equivalent amount of each contract, we multiply this dollar number by a risk weight to produce the final risk-adjusted asset amount for OBS market contracts. In general, the appropriate risk weight is .5, or 50 percent:

$$\begin{array}{l} \text{Risk-adjusted asset value} \\ \text{of OBS market contracts} \end{array} = \begin{array}{l} \text{Total credit equivalent} \\ \text{amount} \times .5 \text{ (risk weight)} \end{array} \quad (13.2)$$

An Example

Suppose that the bank had taken one interest-rate hedging position in the fixed–floating interest rate swap market for 4 years with a notional dollar amount of $100 million, and one 2-year forward $/£ foreign exchange contract for $40 million. The credit equivalent amount for each item or contract is shown in Table 13.2.

For the 4-year fixed–floating interest rate swap, the notional value (contract face value) of the swap is $100 million. Because this is a long-term, over-one-year, less-than-five-years interest rate contract, its face value is multiplied by .005 to get a potential exposure or credit risk equivalent value of $0.5 million (see Table 13.2). We add this potential exposure to the replacement cost (current exposure) of this contract to the bank. The replacement cost reflects the cost of having to enter into a new fixed–floating swap agreement, at today's interest rates, for the remaining life of the swap. Assuming that interest rates today are less favorable, on a present-value basis, the cost of replacing

Table 13.2   Potential Exposure + Current Exposure ($ Millions)

Type of Contract (remaining maturity)	Notional Principal ×	Potential Exposure Conversion Factor =	Potential Exposure ($)	Replacement Cost	Current Exposure =	Credit Equivalent Amount
4-year fixed– floating interest rate swap	$100 ×	.005 =	.5	3	3 =	$3.5
2-year forward foreign exchange contract	$ 40 ×	.05 =	2	–1	0 =	$2

$A_{gross} = \$2.5$ Net current exposure = $2   Current exposure = $3

the existing contract for its remaining life would be $3 million. Thus, the total credit equivalent amount—current plus potential exposure for the interest rate swap—is $3.5 million.

Next, we can look at the foreign exchange 2-year forward contract of $40 million face value. Because this is an over-one-year, less-than-five-years foreign exchange contract, the potential (future) credit risk is $40 million × .05 or $2 million (see Table 13.2). However, its replacement cost is *minus* $1 million, and when the replacement cost of a contract is negative, current exposure has to be set equal to zero (as shown). Thus, the sum of potential exposure ($2 million) and current exposure ($0) produces a total credit equivalent amount of $2 million for this contract.

Because the bank has just two OBS derivative contracts, summing the two credit equivalent amounts produces a total credit equivalent amount of $3.5 million + $2 million = $5.5 million for the bank's OBS market contracts. The next step is to multiply this credit equivalent amount with the appropriate risk weight. Specifically, to calculate the risk-adjusted asset value for the bank's OBS derivative or market contracts, we multiply the credit equivalent amount by the appropriate risk weight, which, for virtually all over-the-counter derivative security products, is .5, or 50 percent:[3]

Risk-adjusted asset value of OBS derivatives = $5.5 million (credit equivalent amount) $\times$ 0.5 (risk weight) = $2.75 million

As with the risk-based capital requirement for loans, the BIS regulations do not directly take into account potential reductions in credit risk from holding a diversified portfolio of OBS contracts. As Hendricks (1994) and others have shown, a portfolio of 50 pay-floating and 50 pay-fixed swap contracts will be less risky than a portfolio of 100 pay-fixed (or floating) contracts (see Appendix 13.2). Nevertheless, although portfolio diversification is not recognized directly, it has been recognized indirectly since October 1995, when banks were allowed to net contracts with the same counterparty under standard master agreements.

The post-1995 rules define net current exposure as the net sum of all positive and negative replacement costs (or mark-to-market values of the individual derivative contracts). The net potential exposure is defined by a formula that adjusts the gross potential exposure estimated earlier:

$$A_{net} = (0.4 \times A_{gross}) + (0.6 \times NGR \times A_{gross})$$

where A_{net} is the net potential exposure (or adjusted sum of potential future credit exposures), A_{gross} is the sum of the potential exposures of each contract, and NGR is the ratio of net current exposure to gross current exposure. The 0.6 is the amount of potential exposure that is reduced as a result of netting.[4]

The same example (without netting) will be used to show the effect of netting on the total credit equivalent amount. Here, we

---

[3] The capital requirement would then be 8 percent of $2.75 million, or $220,000.

[4] See Federal Reserve Board of Governors press release, August 29, 1995, p. 17.

assume both contracts are with the same counterparty (see Table 13.2).

The net current exposure is the sum of the positive and negative replacement costs; that is, +$3 million and −$1 million = $2 million. The gross potential exposure (A_{gross}) is the sum of the individual potential exposures: $2.5 million. To determine the net potential exposure, the following formula is used:

$$A_{net} = (0.4 \times A_{gross}) + (0.6 \times NGR \times A_{gross})$$
$$NGR = \text{Net current exposure/Current exposure} = \tfrac{2}{3} \quad (13.5)$$
$$A_{net} = (0.4 \times 2.5) + (0.6 \times \tfrac{2}{3} \times 2.5)$$
$$= \$2 \text{ million}$$

$$\frac{\text{Total credit}}{\text{equivalent amount}} = \frac{\text{Net potential exposure}}{+\text{Net current exposure}} \quad (13.6)$$
$$\$4 \text{ million} = \$2 \text{ million} + \$2 \text{ million}$$

$$\begin{array}{l}\text{Risk-adjusted asset} \\ \text{value of OBS} \\ \text{market contracts}\end{array} = \begin{array}{l}\text{Total credit} \\ \text{equivalent amount} \\ \times 0.5 \text{ (risk weight)}\end{array} \quad (13.7)$$
$$= \$4 \text{ million} \times 0.5 = \$2 \text{ million}$$

As can be seen, using netting reduces the risk-adjusted asset value from $2.75 million to $2 million. And, given the BIS 8 percent capital requirement, the capital required against the OBS contracts is reduced from $220,000 to $160,000.

CREDITMETRICS AND SWAP CREDIT: VAR

The BIS is concerned with calculating default risk on an OBS instrument, such as a swap, if default were to occur today (current exposure) or at any future time during the contract's remaining

Figure 13.1 Calculating the Forward Value
of a Default Risk-Free Swap

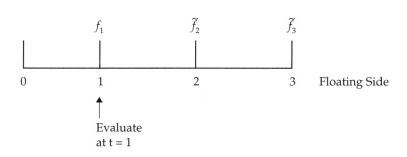

life (potential exposure). CreditMetrics concentrates its VAR calculation on the one-year horizon. Assuming some credit event occurs during the next year, how will the value of the swap be affected during its remaining life?

Conceptually, the value of a swap is the difference between two components. The first component is the NPV of a swap between two default-risk-free counterparties. This involves valuing the swap at the year 1 horizon, based on fixed and expected (forward) government rates, and discounting by the forward zero curve (see Chapter 4, Appendix 4.1).

For example, in a three-year plain-vanilla swap (see Figure 13.1), the expected net present value at the one-year horizon [hereafter, swap future value (FV)] would be:

$$FV = \frac{\overline{F} - \tilde{f}_2}{1 + z'_1} + \frac{\overline{F} - \tilde{f}_3}{\left(1 + z'_2\right)^2} \qquad (13.8)$$

where F = fixed rate on swap,
$\quad \tilde{f}_i$ = forward rates (expected floating rates),
$\quad z'_i$ = forward zero-coupon rates.

Note that any positive (or negative) FV reflects movements in government yield curves and thus interest-rate (or market) risk on the swap rather than the default risk on the swap—although, as noted earlier and in what follows, it is difficult to separate the two because the more out-of-the-money a contract becomes to any given party, the greater is the incentive to default.

The second component is an adjustment for credit-risk. CreditMetrics deducts from the FV of any swap an expected loss amount reflecting credit risk. This expected loss amount will vary by the end of the year-1 horizon-rating category of the counterparty (e.g., AAA versus C) and by default (D). Thus, as with loans, eight different expected losses will be associated with the eight different transition states over the one-year horizon (including the counterparty's credit rating, remaining unchanged). Hence:

$$
\begin{array}{ccc}
\text{Value of} & \text{FV} & \text{Expected loss} \\
\text{swap at} & \text{(risk-free} & \text{rating class R,} \\
\text{year 1 for} = \text{future value} - \text{(year 1 through} \\
\text{rating class R} & \text{in year 1)} & \text{to maturity)}
\end{array}
\qquad (13.9)
$$

In turn, for each of the seven nondefault ratings, the expected loss is calculated as the product of three variables:

$$
\begin{array}{ccccc}
\text{Expected} & \text{Average} & & \text{Cumulative} & \text{Loss} \\
\text{loss} & \text{exposure} & & \text{probability of} & \text{given} \\
\text{(rating} = \text{(year 1} & \times & \text{default (year 1} & \times & \text{default} \\
\text{class R)} & \text{through year } N) & & \text{through year } N) &
\end{array}
\qquad (13.10)
$$

We discuss each variable on the following page.

Average Exposure

As is well known, two general forces drive the default risk exposure on a fixed–floating swap. The first is what may be called the interest-rate diffusion effect—the tendency of floating rates to drift apart from fixed rates with the passage of time. The degree of drift depends on the type of interest rate model employed (e.g., mean reversion or no mean reversion), but, in general, the diffusion effect on exposure may be as shown in Figure 13.2(a): increasing with the term of the swap. Offsetting the diffusion effect, in terms of replacement cost, is the maturity effect. As time passes and the swap gets closer to maturity, the number of payment periods a replacement contract must cover declines. Thus, the maturity effect tends to reduce exposure as the time remaining to swap maturity shrinks [see Figure 13.2(b)]. The overall effect of the two forces on future replacement cost (exposure) is shown in Figure 13.2(c), which suggests that future exposure levels rise, reach a maximum, and then decline. To measure exposure amounts each year into the future, two approaches are normally followed: (1) a Monte Carlo simulation method or (2) an option pricing method.[5]

Figure 13.2(c) shows the average annual exposure amount. For a three-year swap, with two years to run beyond the one-year credit-event horizon, the average exposure is the average of the swap's exposure as measured at the beginning of year 2 and year 3.

---

[5] See Appendix 13.1 and Smith, Smithson, and Wilford (1990). The intuition behind using a Black–Scholes-type model to measure potential exposure can be seen by looking at the five variables that would determine the option value to default on a swap, i.e., the original interest rate on the swap (the strike price), the current interest rate (the current underlying price), the volatility of interest rates (σ), the short-term interest rate (r), and the time to maturity of the swap (τ). That is, $0 = f(s, p, \sigma, r, \tau)$.

Figure 13.2 Measuring Swap Future Exposure

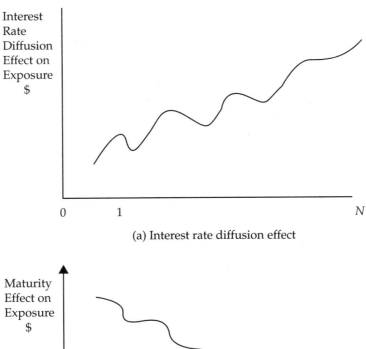

(a) Interest rate diffusion effect

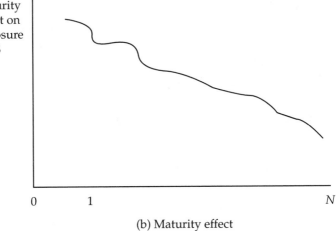

(b) Maturity effect

Figure 13.2 (Continued)

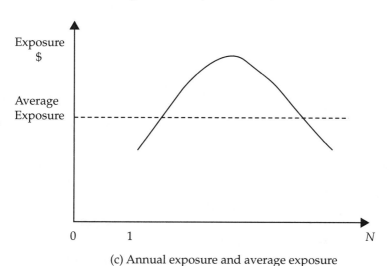

(c) Annual exposure and average exposure

Cumulative Probability of Default

As discussed in Chapter 7, the cumulative mortality rate (CMR) over N years is linked to marginal (annual) mortality rates (MMRs) by:

$$CMR = 1 - \prod_{i=1}^{N} (1 - MMR_i) \qquad (13.11)$$

Assuming that transition probabilities follow a stationary Markov process, then the CMRs for any given rating can be found by either: (1) using a methodology similar to Altman (1989), that is, calculating the annual MMR's and then the appropriate CMR for the remaining life of the swap, or (2) multiplying the annual transition matrix by itself N times (where N is the remaining years of the swap contract at the one-year horizon).[6] In the three-year swap, the cumulative mortality rates would be the last column calculated from the matrix:

$$\begin{bmatrix} \text{One-year} \\ \text{transition matrix} \end{bmatrix}^2 \qquad (13.12)$$

Loss Given Default

The loss given default or (1 − Recovery rate) should not only reflect the loss per contract, but, where relevant (as under the BIS rules), take netting into account.

The product of average exposure (AE), the cumulative probability of default (CMR), and LGD gives the expected loss for each of the seven nondefault rating transitions. For the transition at the credit horizon to default (i.e., during year 1 of the swap), the expected loss is given as:

$$\text{Expected loss on default} = \frac{\text{Expected exposure}}{\text{in year 1}} \times \text{LGD} \qquad (13.13)$$

Specifically, in the three-year swap, where default is assumed to occur at the end of year 1, exposure will be measured by the total replacement cost over the remaining two years of the swap.[7]

An Example

Following CreditMetrics, consider the example of a three-year fixed floating swap with a notional value of $10 million, an LGD of

---

[6] The question, of course, is which transition matrix to use. Arguably, because the cash flows on swaps are similar to the coupon flows on bonds, a bond transition matrix may prove to be adequate.

[7] This is an approximation. Default can occur at any time between time 0 and the end of the 1-year credit-event horizon.

50 percent, and an average exposure, measured at the end of year 1, of $61,627. Based on historical (bond) transition matrices (and CMRs calculated therefrom) for a counterparty rated AA at the end of the one-year credit-event horizon, the value of the swap is:

$$\begin{array}{l} \text{Value of swap at} \\ \text{credit horizon} \end{array} = FV - \text{Expected loss}$$

$$= FV - [AE \times CMR_{AA} \times LGD]$$

$$= FV - [\$61,627 \times .0002 \times .5]$$

$$= FV - \$6$$

For a three-year swap where the counterparty is rated CCC at the end of the one-year credit horizon:

$$\begin{array}{l} \text{Value of swap at} \\ \text{credit horizon} \end{array} = FV - [\$61,627 \times .3344 \times .5]$$

$$= FV - \$10,304$$

The lower value of the CCC counterparty swap reflects the higher CMR of that type of counterparty over the remaining two years of the swap.

For a swap, where the counterparty defaults during the one-year horizon, expected exposure (EE; replacement cost) over the remaining two years is assumed to be $101,721. Thus:

$$\begin{array}{l} \text{Value of swap at} \\ \text{the one-year horizon} \end{array} = FV - [EE \times LGD]$$

$$= FV - [\$101,721 \times .5]$$

$$= FV - \$50,860$$

Table 13.3 summarizes the expected swap values at the end of year 1 under the seven possible rating transitions and the one default state.

The size of the expected and unexpected loss of value on a swap will depend on the initial rating of the counterparty at time

Table 13.3   Value of Three-Year Swap at
the End of Year 1

Rating	Value ($)
AAA	FV −1
AA	FV −6
A	FV −46
BBB	FV −148
BB	FV −797
B	FV −3,209
CCC	FV −10,304
D	FV −50,860

Source: CREDITMETRICS-Technical Document,
April 2, 1997, p. 51.

0 (today), the one-year transition probabilities during the first year, and the one-year forward or expected future values (FV) calculated in Table 13.4, where the counterparty is rated as AA today (time 0).

The credit-related expected loss of value on the swap is $21.8, and the 99 percent unexpected loss of value (VAR) is approximately $126.2. If the original rating of the swap counterparty is lower, the expected and unexpected losses of value are likely to be higher.

A similar methodology could be used to calculate the credit VAR of forwards (swaps can be viewed as a succession of forward contracts) as well as interest rate options and caps. For example, the average exposure on a three-year interest rate cap, as measured at the end of the one-year horizon, would be the average of the replacement cost of the cap (the fair value of the cap premium[8] under an appropriate interest rate model) measured at the beginning of year 2 and the beginning of year 3. As with swaps, replacement costs tend to reflect a similar inverted U-shape, as

---

[8] A cap can be valued as a call option on interest rates or a put on the price of a bond.

Table 13.4 Expected and Unexpected Loss on a Three-Year $10 Million Swap to an AA Counterparty

Rating at Year 1	One-Year Transition Probability (%)	Value of Swap at One-Year Horizon ($)
AAA	0.7	FV −1
AA	90.65	FV −6
A	7.65	FV −46
BBB	0.77	FV −148
BB	0.06	FV −797
B	0.14	FV −3,209
CCC	0.02	FV −10,304
D	0.01	FV −50,860
	100	Expected FV −21.8 Value
		99% Value FV −148

$$\frac{99\% \text{ Unexpected}}{\text{loss of value}} = \left[\text{Expected value} - 99 \text{ percent value}\right] = \$126.2.$$

shown in Figure 13.2(c), because of the offsetting effects of the interest rate diffusion effect and the maturity effect.[9]

SUMMARY

In this chapter, we have analyzed the way in which a VAR-type methodology can be extended to the credit risk of derivative instruments. The BIS model uses a bucketing approach based on the type of contract and its maturity, but newer private-sector models such as CreditMetrics have sought to extend, to the calculation of the credit VAR on derivative instruments, a methodology similar to that used in loan valuation and VAR calculation.

---

[9] CreditMetrics currently allows for the estimation of the VAR for OBS activities, such as loan commitments and credit guarantees (such as letters of credit). Reportedly, it will soon be adding a routine to calculate the VAR of Asset-Backed Securities as well.

Appendix **13.1**

BIS Model

SIMULATION STEPS

1. Choose a random number between 0 and 1. Set this equal to ϕ (z), the area under the standard normal cumulative density function (c.d.f.) to the left of the level z.
2. Look up z for this value of ϕ (z) from the standard normal c.d.f. table.
3. $\Delta(\log r) = z \dfrac{s}{\sqrt{2}}$, i.e., assumed log-normal interest rate process.
4. $\log R_{i+1} = \log R_i + \Delta (\log r)$
5. $R_{i+1} = \exp (\log R_{i+1})$.
6. Semiannual cash flows.

Example

$$\Delta \log r \sim N(0, s^2 / 2)$$

$$\frac{\sqrt{2}}{s} \Delta \log r \sim N(0,1)$$

$$\phi(z) = P_r\left(\frac{\sqrt{2}}{s} \Delta \log r \le z\right) = P_r\left(\Delta \log r \le z \frac{s}{\sqrt{2}}\right)$$

For additional information, see, Bank of England and Board of Governors of the Federal Reserve System, *Potential Credit Exposure on Interest Rate and Foreign Exchange Rate Related Instruments*, March 1987.

Initial conditions: $R_0 = 0.09$, $s = 0.182$, where s = annual standard deviation of interest rate changes.

Step 1, Simulation 1

$$\log R_{i+1} = \log R_i + \Delta \log r$$

$$= \log(.09) + z\left(\frac{s}{\sqrt{2}}\right)$$

$$= -2.407 + \left[1.127\left(\frac{.182}{1.414}\right)\right]$$

$$= -2.407 + .1449$$

$$= -2.26.$$

$$R_{i+1} = \exp\left[\log R_{i+1}\right] = e^{-2.26}$$

$$= .1043 \text{ or } 10.4 \text{ percent}$$

See line 1, Simulation 1, in Table 13.1A.

Table 13.1A   Monte Carlo Simulation of Future Interest Rates on Fixed–Floating U.S. Interest Rate Swap

	Simulation 1			
R_i	$\phi(z)$ (Random No.)	z	$\Delta \log r_i$	R_{i+1}
$R_0 = 0.09$	0.87	1.127	0.1449	0.1043
$R_1 = 0.1043$	0.33	−0.44	−0.0566	0.0983
$R_2 = 0.0983$	0.18	−0.915	−0.1178	0.0874
$R_3 = 0.0874$	0.24	−0.706	−0.0909	0.0798
$R_4 = 0.0798$	0.42	−0.202	−0.0260	0.0778
$R_5 = 0.0778$	—	—	—	—

	Simulation 2			
R_i	$\phi(z)$ (Random No.)	z	$\Delta \log r_i$	R_{i+1}
$R_0 = 0.09$	0.28	−0.583	−0.075	0.0835
$R_1 = 0.835$	0.91	1.341	0.1726	0.0992
$R_2 = 0.0992$	0.66	0.412	0.0530	0.1046
$R_3 = 0.1046$	0.15	−1.036	−0.1333	0.0916
$R_4 = 0.0916$	0.98	2.054	0.2643	0.1193
$R_5 = 0.1193$	—	—	—	—

Figure 13.1A   Simulating Loss Distributions: Simulation 1

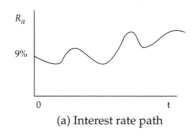

(a) Interest rate path

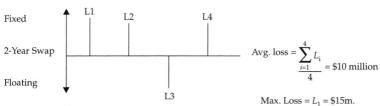

(b) Net losses (L_i) on two back-to-back 2-year I.R. Swaps (semi-annual cash-flows).

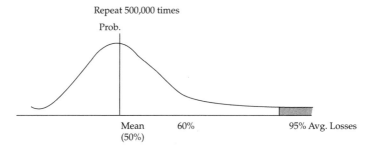

(c) Distribution of average losses

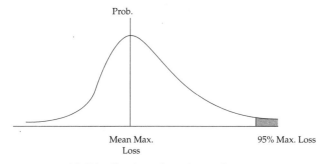

(d) Distribution of maximum losses

Appendix **13.2**

The Effects of Diversification on Swap Portfolio Risk

A simple example, following Hendricks (1994), can demonstrate the risk of a portfolio of swaps and the effects of diversification.

Suppose there are N contracts in the portfolio and the risk (σ_i) of each is the same. Following MPT, the risk of a portfolio (σ_p) is:

$$\sigma_p = \sigma_i \sqrt{N + 2\sum_{\substack{i=1 \\ i \neq j}}^{N}\sum_{j=1}^{N} \rho_{ij}} \qquad (13.1A)$$

Define an average correlation coefficient ($\overline{\rho}$):

$$\overline{\rho} = \frac{\displaystyle\sum_{i=1}^{N}\sum_{j=1}^{N} \rho_{ij}}{\left(N^2 - N\right)/2} \qquad (13.2A)$$

Then

$$\sigma_p = \sigma_i \sqrt{N + \left(N^2 - N\right)\overline{\rho}} \qquad (13.3A)$$

From equation (13.3A), the higher the risk (σ_i) of each swap contract, the higher the risk of the swap portfolio; the larger the number of contracts *(N)* in the portfolio, the higher the risk of the portfolio; and the lower the average correlation coefficient ($\bar{\rho}$), the lower the portfolio risk. Because a more diverse swap portfolio will have a lower $\bar{\rho}$ (e.g., an equal mix of pay fixed/receive floating, and pay floating/receive fixed), the composition of the swap portfolio may be as important as its size in determining the credit risk of an OBS derivatives portfolio.

Chapter 14

Credit Derivatives

INTRODUCTION

In recent years, there has been an explosive growth in the use of credit derivatives. A Canadian Imperial Bank of Commerce (CIBC) survey, in May 1996, put the market at around $40 billion in notional value. The recent crisis in emerging markets and its adverse effects on banks have apparently resulted in a further rise in usage. According to *Financial Times*,[1] a British Bankers Association survey predicted that the notional value of credit derivatives outstanding would be over $700 billion by the year 2000.

In this chapter, we first document the treatment of credit derivatives under the BIS capital standards, and the use of these instruments in solving the "paradox of credit." We then look at the individual instruments: (1) credit options, (2) credit swaps, (3) credit forwards, and (4) credit securitizations.

CREDIT DERIVATIVES AND THE BIS CAPITAL REQUIREMENTS

The role of credit derivatives in credit risk management can best be seen in the context of the paradox of credit, discussed in

---

[1] "The Growth of Credit Derivatives?" *Financial Times*, London, October 7, 1998, p. 1.

Chapter 9 (see Figure 9.1). Given a concentrated loan portfolio, there are at least two ways to reach the efficient frontier and/or improve its risk–return performance. The first, as discussed in Chapters 9 and 10, is to more actively manage the loan portfolio by trading loans. However, as noted in Chapter 9, this tends to adversely impact customer relationships, especially if a long-term borrower from a bank discovers that his or her loan has been sold.

An alternate way to improve the risk–return trade-off on a loan portfolio is to take an off-balance-sheet position in credit derivatives. As will be discussed below, credit derivatives allow a bank to alter the risk–return trade-off of a loan portfolio without having to sell or remove loans from the balance sheet. Apart from avoiding an adverse customer relationship effect, the use of credit derivatives (rather than loan sales) may allow a bank to avoid adverse timing of tax payments, as well as liquidity problems related to buying back a similar loan at a later date if risk–return considerations so dictate. Thus, for customer relationship, tax, transaction cost, and liquidity reasons, a bank may prefer the credit derivative solution to loan portfolio optimization rather than the more direct (loan trading) portfolio management solution.

Despite their apparent value as credit risk management tools, credit derivatives have not been well treated under the BIS capital requirements. According to Wall and Shrikhande (1998), the present U.S. approach is to treat credit derivatives as a loan guarantee, provided the payoff from the credit derivative is sufficiently highly correlated with the loan. If the counterparty is neither a bank nor a government entity, the risk weight is 100 percent; no risk reduction is recognized. If the counterparty is a bank, the risk weight on the loan for the buyer of the guarantee is 20 percent; however, for the bank that issues the guarantee to the counterparty, the risk weight of the guarantee is 100 percent (i.e., it's as if the counterparty has been extended a loan). Thus, in aggregate, the combined risk-based capital requirements of the two banks could increase as a result of using the derivative. (Under certain conditions, however, this capital burden may be reduced.[2])

Next, we look at how various types of derivatives can be used to hedge the credit risk of loans or portfolios of loans.

HEDGING CREDIT RISK WITH OPTIONS

The rationale for using option contracts was detailed in Chapter 3, where it was argued that a banker, in making a loan, receives a payoff similar to that of a writer of a put option on the assets of a firm. The upside return on the loan is relatively fixed (as is the premium to a put option writer) and has a long-tailed downside risk (like the potential payout exposure of a put option writer; see Figure 14.1). If a banker making a loan faces a risk equivalent to writing a put option on the assets of the firm, he or she may seek to hedge that risk by buying a put option on the assets of the firm, so as to truncate or limit a part, or all, of the downside risk on the loan (or portfolio of loans).

One early use of options in this context was for farming loans in the Midwest. In return for a loan, a wheat farmer was required to post collateral in the form of put options on wheat purchased from a major Chicago options exchange. If the price of wheat fell,

---

[2] Wall and Shrikhande (1998) note that "the combined regulatory capital requirements may be reduced if three conditions are met: (1) the bank selling the credit risk is bound by the risk-based guidelines, (2) the counterparty's (the buyer of the credit risk) required capital under the leverage standard exceeds its required capital under the risk-based standard, and (3) the counterparty does not already have such a high level of off-balance-sheet commitments that the regulators impose a judgmental increase in its leverage requirement. In this case, the bank holding the loan and selling its risk would reduce its capital requirement for the loan to one-fifth the original level (moving from a 100 percent weighting to a 20 percent weighting). Further, the counterparty may not experience any increase in its capital requirements since the credit derivative would not be included in the calculation of its leverage ratio" (p. 10).

Figure 14.1 Hedging the Risk on a Loan to a Wheat Farmer

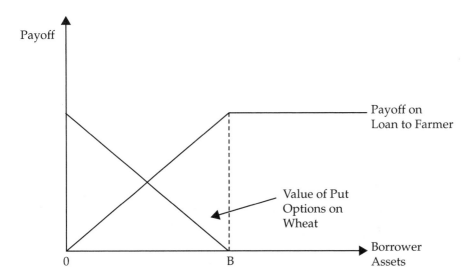

the market value of the loan fell because the probability of the farmer's repaying the loan in full declined (and the LGD increased). Offsetting this decline in the implied market value of the loan was the rise in value of the put options on wheat posted as collateral by the borrower. The offsetting effect of the rising value of the wheat put options is shown in Figure 14.1.

There are two problems with this type of hedging vehicle:

1. The farmer may default for idiosyncratic reasons (e.g., divorce, injury, and so on) rather than because the price of the crop falls. As a result, a large "basis risk" is present in the hedge.

2. The requirement that the farmer must post collateral (and thus pay an options premium to the exchange) may make the loan contract very expensive—especially if the farmer is required to buy close-to-the-money options—and may harm the bank's relationship with the farmer.

In recent years, more direct methods of hedging credit risk through options have been developed. A *credit spread call option* is a call option on which the payoff increases as the credit spread on a borrower's specified benchmark bond increases above some exercise spread, S_T. If a bank is concerned that the risk of a loan will increase, it can purchase a credit spread call option to hedge its increased credit risk. (See Figure 14.2.) As the credit quality of a borrower declines, his or her bond credit spread rises, and the potential payoffs from the option increase. To the extent the values of the borrower's (nontraded) loans and publicly traded bonds are highly correlated, the decline in the value of the loan (as credit quality declines) is offset by the increase in the value of the option.[3] Specifically, the payoff from the spread option will be:

$$\text{Payoff on option} = MD \times \text{Face value of option} \times [\text{Current credit spread} - S_T] \quad (14.1)$$

where MD = the modified duration of the underlying bond in the credit spread option contract;
S_T = the strike spread.[4]

A second innovation is the *default option*, an option that pays a stated amount in the event of a loan default (the extreme case of increased credit risk). As shown in Figure 14.3, the bank can purchase a default option covering the par value of a loan (or loans) in its portfolio. In the event of a loan default, the option writer pays the bank the par value of the defaulted loans. If the loans are paid off in accordance with the loan agreement, however, the default option expires unexercised. As a result, the bank will suffer a maximum loss on the option equal to the premium (cost) of buying the default option from the writer (seller). There are other variants on

---

[3] We have shown payoffs on the loan as piecewise linear in reality the loan payoff will have some convexity.

[4] For additional discussion, see Finnerty (1996).

Figure 14.2 The Payoff of a Credit Spread Option

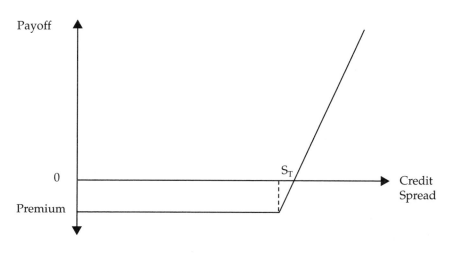

Figure 14.3 A Default Option

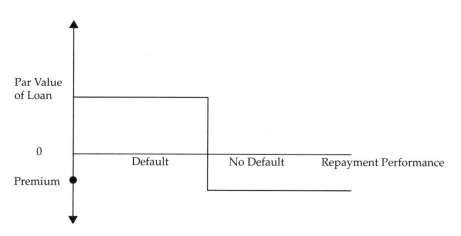

these simple options; for example, a barrier feature might be written into the credit spread option. If the credit quality of a borrower improves, and spreads fall below some "barrier" spread, the option will cease to exist. In return, the buyer of the credit spread option will pay a lower premium than would be required for the plain-vanilla credit spread option considered above.

HEDGING CREDIT RISK WITH SWAPS

Credit options are being used increasingly, but the dominant credit derivative to date has been the credit swap. There are two main types of credit swap: (1) total return swap and (2) pure credit or default swap.

The Total Return Swap

A total return swap involves swapping an obligation to pay interest at a specified fixed or floating rate for payments representing the total return on a loan or a bond. (Interest, fees, and market value change.)

For example, suppose that a bank lends $100 million to a manufacturing firm at a fixed rate of 10 percent. If the firm's credit risk increases unexpectedly over the life of the loan, the market value of the loan will fall. The bank can seek to hedge an unexpected increase in the borrower's credit risk by entering into a total return swap in which it agrees to pay a counterparty the total return based on an annual rate $(\overline{F})$ equal to the promised interest (and fees) on the loan, plus the change in the market value of the loan. In return, the bank receives a variable market rate payment of interest annually [e.g., one-year LIBOR (London Interbank Offered Rate) that reflects its cost of funds]. Figure 14.4 and Table 14.1 illustrate the cash flows associated with the typical total return swap.

Using the total return swap, the bank agrees to pay a fixed rate of interest annually, plus the capital gains or losses on the

Figure 14.4 Cash Flows on Total Return Swap

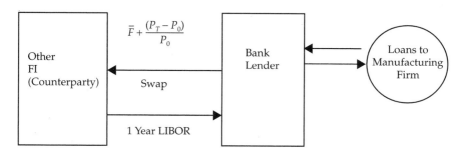

market value of the loan over the period of the swap. In Figure 14.4, P_0 denotes the market value of the loan at the beginning of the swap payment period, and P_T represents the market value of the loan at the end of a swap payment period (here, one year). If the loan decreases in value over the payment period, the bank pays the counterparty a relatively small (possibly negative) amount equal to the fixed payment on the swap minus the capital

Table 14.1 Cash Flows on Total Return Swap

	Annual Cash Flow for Year 1 through Final Year	Additional Payment by FI	Total Return (First Payment Period)
Cash inflow (on swap to bank)	1 year LIBOR (11 percent)	—	1 year LIBOR (11 percent)
Cash outflow (on swap to FI)	Fixed rate $(\bar{F})$ (12 percent)	$\dfrac{P_T - P_0}{P_0}$	$\bar{F} + \left[\dfrac{P_T - P_0}{P_0}\right]$
			12 percent $+ \dfrac{90 - 100}{100} =$
			12 percent $-$ 10 percent $=$ 2 percent
			Net profit $=$ 11 percent $-$ 2 percent
			$=$ 9 percent

loss[5] on the loan. For example, suppose the loan was priced at par ($P_0 = 100$) at the beginning of the swap period. At the end of the swap period (or the first payment date), the loan has an estimated market value of 90 ($P_T = 90$) because of an increase in the borrower's credit risk. Suppose that the fixed rate payment $(\overline{F})$ as part of the total return swap is 12 percent. The bank would send to the swap counterparty the fixed rate of 12 percent minus 10 percent (the capital loss on the loan), or a total of 2 percent, and would receive in return a floating payment (e.g., LIBOR = 11 percent) from the counterparty to the swap. Thus, the net profit on the swap to the bank/lender is 9 percent (11 percent minus 2 percent) times the notional amount of the swap contract. This gain can be used to offset the loss of market value of the loan over that period. This example is summarized in Table 14.1.[6]

Pure Credit or Default Swaps

Total return swaps can be used to hedge credit risk exposure, but they contain an element of interest (or market) risk as well as credit risk. For example, in Table 14.1, if the LIBOR rate changes, then the *net* cash flows on the total return swap will also change, even though the credit risk of the underlying loans has not necessarily changed.

To strip out the interest-rate-sensitive element of total return swaps, an alternate swap, called a "pure" credit or default swap, has been developed.

As shown in Figure 14.5, the bank lender will send (in each swap period) a fixed fee or payment (similar to an option premium) to the bank or FI counterparty. If the bank lender's loan

---

[5] Total return swaps are typically structured so that the capital gain or loss is paid at the end of the swap. However, in the alternate structure used in this example, the capital gain or loss is paid at the end of each interest period during the swap.

[6] For additional discussion, see Finnerty (1996).

Figure 14.5   A Pure Credit Swap

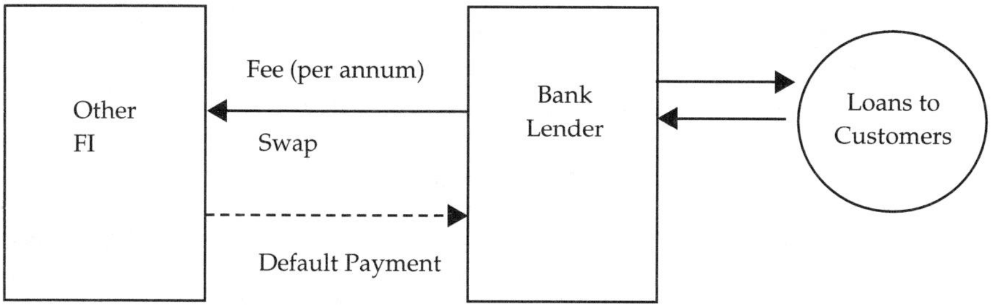

(or loans) does not default, it will receive nothing back from the swap counterparty. However, if the loan (or loans) defaults, the counterparty will cover the default loss by making a default payment equal to the par value of the original loan (e.g., $P_0 = \$100$) minus the secondary market value of the defaulted loan (e.g., $P_T = \$40$); i.e., the counterparty will pay the bank $P_0 - P_T$ ($\$60$, in this example).[7, 8] A pure credit swap is like buying credit insurance and/or a multiperiod credit option.

HEDGING CREDIT RISK WITH CREDIT FORWARDS

A *credit forward* is a forward agreement that hedges against an increase in default risk on a loan (decline in credit quality of a

---

[7] A pure credit swap is like a default option (e.g., see the earlier discussion), but a key difference is that the fee (or premium) payments on the swap are paid over the life of the swap, whereas for a default option the whole fee (premium) is paid upfront.

[8] Default payments are usually computed in one of three ways: (1) par minus a final loan price as determined by a dealer poll; (2) payment of par by the counterparty in exchange for physical delivery of the defaulted loan; and (3) a fixed dollar amount contractually agreed to at the swap origination. Increasingly, method (2) is the favored method of settlement because of the difficulty in getting accurate secondary market prices on loans around credit event dates.

borrower) after the loan rate is determined and the loan has been issued. The credit forward agreement specifies a credit spread (a risk premium above the risk-free rate, to compensate for default risk) on a benchmark bond issued by the (loan) borrower. For example, suppose the benchmark bond of the borrower was rated BBB at the time a loan was originated from a bank, and it had an interest spread over a U.S. Treasury bond of the same maturity of 2 percent. Then $S_F = 2$ percent defines the credit spread on which the credit forward contract is written. Figure 14.6 illustrates the payment pattern on a credit forward. S_T is the actual credit spread on the bond when the credit forward matures (e.g., one year after the loan was originated and the credit forward contract was entered into); MD is the modified duration on the benchmark BBB bond; and A is the principal amount of the forward agreement.

The payment pattern established in a credit forward agreement is detailed in Figure 14.6. The credit forward buyer bears the risk of an increase in default risk on the benchmark bond of the borrowing firm, and the credit forward seller (the bank lender) hedges itself against an increase in the borrower's default risk. Suppose the borrower's default risk increases so that when the forward agreement matures the market requires a higher

Figure 14.6   Payment Pattern on a Credit Forward Agreement

Credit Spread at End of Forward Agreement	Credit Spread: Seller (Bank)	Credit Spread: Buyer (Counterparty)
$S_T > S_F$	Receives $(S_T - S_F) \times MD \times A$	Pays $(S_T - S_F) \times MD \times A$
$S_F > S_T$	Pays $(S_F - S_T) \times MD \times A$	Receives $(S_F - S_T) \times MD \times A$

Figure 14.7   Payoff on a Credit Forward Contract

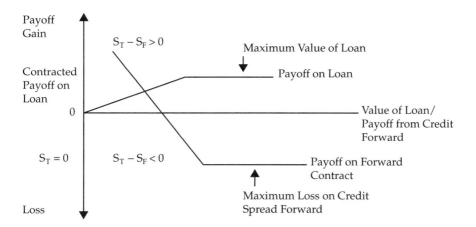

credit spread on the borrower's benchmark bond (S_T) than was originally agreed to in the forward contract (S_F) (i.e., $S_T > S_F$). The credit forward buyer then pays the credit forward seller (the bank): ($S_T - S_F$) × MD × A. For example, suppose the credit spread between BBB bonds and U.S. Treasury bonds widened to 3 percent from 2 percent over the year, the modified duration (MD) of the benchmark BBB bond was 5 years, and the size of the forward contract (A) was $10,000,000. The gain on the credit forward contract to the seller (the bank) would then be (3% – 2%) × 5 × $10,000,000 = $500,000. This amount could be used to offset the loss in market value of the loan due to the rise in the borrower's default risk. If the borrower's default risk and credit spread decrease over the year, the credit forward seller pays the credit forward buyer: ($S_F - S_T$) × MD × A. [However, the maximum loss on the forward contract (to the bank seller) is limited, as will be explained below.]

Figure 14.7 illustrates the impact on the bank from hedging the loan.[9] If the default risk on the loan increases, the value of the

---

[9] For additional discussion, see Finnerty (1996).

loan falls below its value at the beginning of the hedge period. However, the bank hedged the change in default risk by selling a credit forward contract. Assuming the credit spread on the borrower's benchmark bond also increases (so that $S_T > S_F$), the bank receives $(S_T - S_F) \times MD \times A$ on the forward contract. If the characteristics of the benchmark bond (i.e., credit spread, modified duration, and principal value) are the same as those of the loan to the borrower, the market value loss on the bank's balance sheet is offset completely by the gain from the credit forward. (In our example, a $500,000 market value loss in the loan would be offset by a $500,000 gain from selling the credit forward contract.)

If the default risk does not increase or decreases (so the $S_T < S_F$), the bank selling the forward contract will pay $(S_F - S_T) \times MD \times A$ to the credit forward buyer. However, *this payout by the bank is limited to a maximum.* When S_T falls to zero—i.e., the default spread on BBB bonds falls to zero, or the original BBB bonds of the borrower are viewed as having the same default risk as government bonds (the rate on the benchmark bond is equal to the risk-free rate)—the maximum loss on the credit forward, $[S_F - (0)] \times MD \times A$, offsets the maximum and limited upside gain (return) on the loan. Anyone familiar with options will recognize that, in selling a credit forward, the payoff is similar to buying a put option.

CREDIT SECURITIZATIONS

Until recently, the growth of commercial credit or loan securitization (as in the case of loan sales and trading) had been hampered by concerns about negative customer relationship effects if loans were removed from the balance sheet and packaged and sold as CLOs (collateralized lending obligations) to outside investors. Instead, such mechanisms have proved to be popular for more commoditized credits such as mortgages, credit card loans, and auto loans. Thus, until recently, many loan securitizations were conducted in which loans remained on the balance sheet, and asset-backed securities (credit-linked notes, or CLNs) were issued against the loan portfolio. A huge variety of these products has emerged, but the differences among them relate to the way in which credit risk is transferred from the loan-originating bank to the note investor. In general, a subportfolio of commercial loans is segmented on the asset side of the balance sheet, and an issue of CLNs is made. The return and risk of investors vary by type of issue. Some investors are promised a high yield on the underlying loans in return for bearing all the default risk; other investors are offered lower yields in return for partial default protection (i.e., a shared credit risk with the bank). In general, the bank issuer takes the first tranche of default risk but is protected against catastrophic risk (which is borne by the CLN investor).

In more complex arrangements, a form of double securitization takes place. Loans on the bank's portfolio are segregated, and CLNs are issued against them. Then, as in the August 1997 $1.5-billion deal arranged by the Swiss Bank Corporation (SBC), the CLNs are securitized by being sold to a special-purpose vehicle (SPV; Glacier Funding in the SBC case), which issues bonds backed by CLNs to final investors. A simplified structure of SBC's double securitization of $1.5 billion of its loan portfolio is shown in Figure 14.8. Each CLN was backed by a diversified pool of loans. The CLNs were sold to the SPV (Glacier Funding) and an equivalent amount of bonds was issued to investors in the market. The bank hedged itself against loan default risk in that, if the loans in the bank's subportfolio backing the CLNs defaulted, it could redeem the CLNs sold to the SPV at either 51 percent of face value or the "market price" of the reference security.[10] This effectively passed the credit risk of loans to the holders of the bonds issued

---

[10] The loans underlying the CLN were kept confidential by SBC.

Figure 14.8 Basic Structure of a CLN Securitization

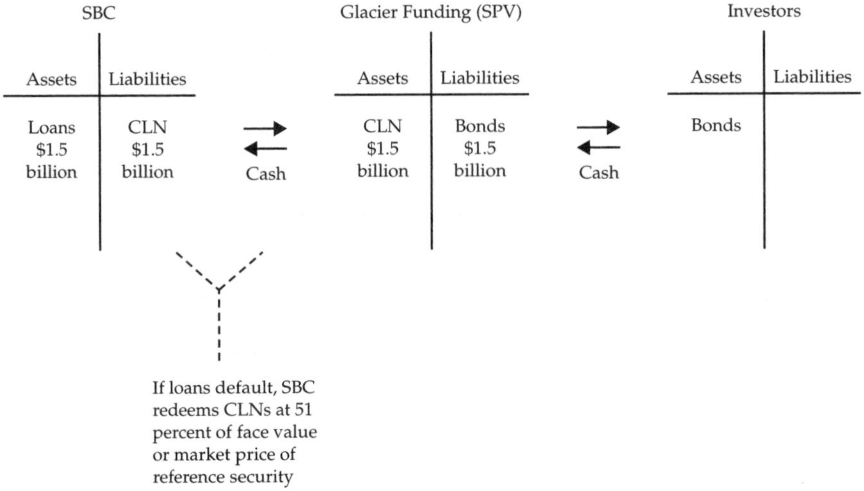

SBC				Glacier Funding (SPV)				Investors	
Assets	Liabilities			Assets	Liabilities			Assets	Liabilities
Loans $1.5 billion	CLN $1.5 billion			CLN $1.5 billion	Bonds $1.5 billion			Bonds	

If loans default, SBC redeems CLNs at 51 percent of face value or market price of reference security

by the SPV. As a result, credit risk (but not the loans themselves) was largely removed from the bank's balance sheet.[11, 12]

PRICING ISSUES

A key question is: What role do the new models play in the credit derivatives market? Apart from identifying counterparty risk, they play a role in pricing. Consider the case of the pure credit swap, discussed earlier. On origination, the NPV of the swap should be zero; that is, the present value of the annual

[11] See Press Release, SBC Warburg, Dillon, Read, "Swiss Bank Corporation launches $1.5 billion securities-backed credit linked notes to securitize part of its credit portfolio risk," August 27, 1997.

[12] Many credit or loan securitizations appear to be driven by regulatory arbitrage, depending on regulatory treatment of such securitizations as well as the difference between the regulatory and the market view of capital sufficiency.

(semiannual) premiums paid by the buyer of credit insurance should equal the present value of expected default losses (probability of default $\times$ LGD) over the swap period. A number of different approaches appear to be used in practice. One approach is to use a KMV-type model to generate EDFs for each future swap date and (combined with LGDs) a projected series of expected losses on the swap. Given a set of appropriate discount rates, the theoretically fair annual premium (annuity) to be paid by the credit risk seller can be established. Unfortunately, this would likely misprice the swap since EDFs are based on historic data, whereas for pricing purposes, we need expectations of future default rates using risk neutral probabilities (see Chapter 6). Since the premium is like a credit spread, resort can be made to models of the term structure of credit spreads, such as Jarrow, Lando, and Turnbull (1997). An alternative approach is to replicate the cash flows of a default swap by replicating its payoffs in the cash market. This assumes instruments in the cash (bond) market are efficiently priced. An example of Merrill Lynch's cash-market replication approach is discussed in the Appendix to this chapter.[13]

SUMMARY

This chapter has looked at the role that credit derivatives are playing in allowing banks to hedge the credit risk of their loan portfolios. The BIS capital requirements do not actively encourage the use of credit derivatives, but banks are attracted to them because of their potential in improving loan return–risk trade-offs without harming customer relationships. Some simple examples of credit options, credit swaps, credit forwards, and credit securitizations were discussed, as was the issue of credit derivative pricing.

---

[13] Currently, the cash replication approach appears to be the most used. Credit spread models appear to be used more to "benchmark" the premium calculated *via* cash replication models.

Appendix **14.1**

Cash Market Replication to Price/Value a Pure Credit or Default Swap

The idea here is that the expected value of credit risk (in a credit swap) is already captured by credit spreads in the cash market for bonds and the market for fixed-floating rate swaps. Figure 14.1A (from Merrill Lynch) shows how the risk on a pure credit swap can be replicated through cash market transactions and plain-vanilla swap transactions where the "investor" sells protection under a pure credit swap.

In this replication, the investor (swap risk seller):

1. Purchases a cash bond with a spread of $T + S_C$ for par,
2. Pays fixed on a swap $(T + S_S)$ with the maturity of the cash bond and receives LIBOR (L),
3. Finances the position in the Repo (repurchase agreement) market [the Repo rate is quoted at a spread to LIBOR $(L - x)$],
4. Pledges the corporate bond as collateral and is charged a "haircut" by the Repo counterparty.

Transactions 1 and 2 hedge the underlying "interest rate" risk involved in purchasing the corporate bond (since we are concerned

---

For more details on this topic, see Merrill Lynch, *Credit Default Swaps*, Global Fixed Income Research, October 1998.

Figure 14.1A   Replicating Default Swap Exposure,
Protection for the Swap Seller

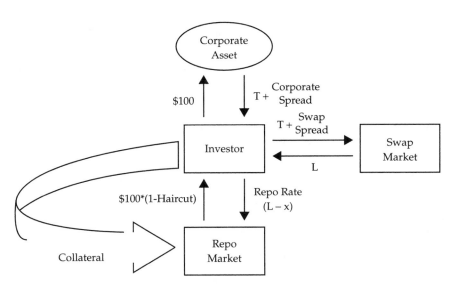

Source: Credit Default Swaps, Merrill Lynch, Pierce, Fenner, and Smith, Inc.,
October 1998, p. 12.

**Table 14.1A   Cash Flows of Default
Swap Replication**

	Receive	Pay
Cash bond	$T+Sc$	$100
Swap hedge	L	$T+Ss$
Repo transaction	$100	$(L-x)$
	$Sc-Ss+x$	

Sc = corporate spreads; Ss = swap spread. Assume no
"haircut."

Source: Credit Default Swaps, Merrill Lynch, Pierce,
Fenner, and Smith, Inc., October 1998, p. 13.

with only credit risk exposure). Transactions 3 and 4 reflect the cost of financing the purchase of the risky corporate bond through the Repo market, where a lender charges a collateral "haircut" on the amount borrowed and $L - x$ reflects the cost of Repo finance. Table 14.1A shows the net cash flows of the four transactions (with the collateral "haircut" set equal to zero for simplicity).

The credit risk exposure of the swap seller (via replication) equals $(S_C - S_S) + x$, i.e., the spread between the corporate bond risk premium and the swap spread in the fixed-floating swap market, plus an amount x that reflects the degree to which the investor can borrow below LIBOR in the Repo market. If $x = 0$, then the credit exposure is $S_C - S_S$, which is analytically equivalent to the (fair) premium or fee that has to be paid to the seller of credit risk insurance in a pure credit (or default) swap transaction, in return for providing default risk insurance.

Bibliography

Acharya, V.V., and J.N. Carpenter, "Callable Defautable Bonds: Valuation, Hedging and Optimal Exercise Boundaries," Working Paper, Dept. of Finance, NYU, March 15, 1999.

Aguais, S.D., L. Forest, S. Krishnamoorthy, and T. Mueller, "Creating Value from Both Loan Structure and Price." *Commercial Lending Review*, 1997, pp. 1–10 (Winter).

Altman, E.I., "Financial Ratios, Discriminant Analysis and the Prediction of Corporate Bankruptcy." *Journal of Finance*, September 1968, pp. 589–609.

Altman, E.I., "Measuring Corporate Bond Mortality and Performance." *Journal of Finance*, September 1989, pp. 909–922.

Altman, E.I., "Predicting Financial Distress of Companies: Revisiting the Z-Score and Zeta Models." Working Paper, NYU Salomon Center, June 1995.

Altman, E.I., T.K.N. Baidya, and L.M.R. Dias, "Assessing Potential Financial Problems for Firms in Brazil." Working Paper 125, NYU Salomon Center, September 1977.

Altman, E.I., and D.L. Kao, "The Implications of Corporate Bond Ratings Drift." *Financial Analysts Journal*, May–June 1992, pp. 64–75.

Altman, E.I., and V.M. Kishore, "Defaults and Returns on High-Yield Bonds: Analysis Through 1997." Working Paper, NYU Salomon Center, January 1998.

Altman, E.I., and P. Narayanan, "An International Survey of Business Failure Classification Models." *Financial Markets, Instruments and Institutions*, Vol. 6, No. 2, 1997.

Altman, E.I., and A. Saunders, "Credit Risk Measurement: Developments over the Last Twenty Years." *Journal of Banking and Finance*, December 1997, pp. 1721–1742.

Altman, E.I., and H.J. Suggitt, "Default Rates in the Syndicated Loan Market: A Mortality Analysis." Working Paper S-97-39, NYU Salomon Center, December 1997.

Anderson, R., and S. Sunderesan, "A Comparative Study of Structural Models of Corporate Bond Yields." Paper presented at Center for Economic Policy Research (CEPR) Conference, London, September 20, 1998.

Anderson, R., S. Sunderesan, and P. Tychon, "Strategic Analysis of Contingent Claims." *European Economic Review*, 1996, pp. 871–881.

Angbazo, L., J-P. Mei, and A. Saunders, "Credit Spreads in the Market for Highly Leveraged Transaction Loans." *Journal of Banking and Finance*, December 1998, pp. 1249–1282.

Arrow, K.K., "Le Rôle des Valeurs Boursieres pour la Repartition de la Meilleure des Risques." Econometrie Colloq. ICNRS, 40, 1953, pp. 41–47.

Asarnow, E., "Managing Bank Loan Portfolios for Total Return." Paper presented at a conference on "A New Market Equilibrium for the Credit Business," Frankfurt, Germany, March 11, 1999.

Asarnow, E., and J. Marker, "Historical Performance of the U.S. Corporate Loan Market, 1988–1993." *Journal of Commercial Lending*, Spring 1995, pp. 13–22.

Asquith, P., D.W. Mullins, and E.D. Wolff, "Original Issue High Yield Bonds: Aging Analysis of Defaults, Exchanges and Calls." *Journal of Finance*, September 1989, pp. 923–952.

Babbel, D.F., "Insuring Banks Against Systematic Credit Risk." *Journal of Futures Markets*, November 6, 1989, pp. 487–506.

Bank for International Settlements, *Standardized Model for Market Risk.* Basle, Switzerland: Bank for International Settlements, 1996.

Belkin, B., L.R. Forest, S.D. Aguais, and S.J. Suchower, "Credit Risk Premiums in Commercial Lending (I)." KPMG, New York, August 1998a (mimeo).

Belkin, B., L.R. Forest, S.D. Aguais, and S.J. Suchower, "Credit Risk Premiums in Commercial Lending (II)." KPMG, New York, August 1998b (mimeo).

Belkin, B., S.J. Suchower, and L.R. Forest, "The Effect of Systematic Credit Risk on Loan Portfolio Value at Risk and Loan Pricing." *CreditMetrics Monitor*, 1998c, pp. 17–28.

Belkin, B., S.J. Suchower, D.H. Wagner, and L.R. Forest, "Measures of Credit Risk and Loan Value in LAS^{SM}." KPMG Risk Strategy Practice, 1998d (mimeo).

Black, F., and M. Scholes, "The Pricing of Options and Corporate Liabilities." *Journal of Political Economy*, May–June 1973, pp. 637–654.

Boudoukh, J., M. Richardson, and R. Whitelaw, "Expect the Worst." *Risk Magazine*, September 1995, pp. 101–105.

Brenner, M., and Y.H. Eom, "No Arbitrage Option Pricing: New Evidence on the Validity of the Martingale Property." Working Paper 97-10, NYU Salomon Center, 1997.

Caouette, J.B., E.J. Altman, and P. Narayanan, *Managing Credit Risk: The Next Great Financial Challenge*. John Wiley & Sons, New York, 1998.

Carey, M., "Credit Risk in Private Debt Portfolios." *Journal of Finance*, August 1998, pp. 1363–1387.

Carey, M., M. Post, and S.A. Sharpe, "Does Corporate Lending by Banks and Finance Companies Differ? Evidence on Specialization in Private Debt Contracting." *Journal of Finance*, Vol. 53, June 1998, pp. 845–878.

Carty, L.V., and D. Lieberman, "Corporate Bond Defaults and Default Rates 1938–1995." Moody's Investors Service, Global Credit Research, January 1996.

Carty, L.V., and D. Lieberman, "Defaulted Bank Loan Recoveries." Moody's Investors Service, Global Credit Research (Special Report), 1996.

Choudhury, S.P., "Choosing the Right Box of Credit Tricks." *Risk Magazine*, November 1997, pp. 17–22.

Coates, P.K., and L.F. Fant, "Recognizing Financial Distress Patterns Using a Neural Network Tool." *Financial Management*, Summer 1993, pp. 142–155.

Crédit Suisse Financial Products, "Credit Risk Plus." Technical Document, London/New York, October 1997.

Crouhy, M., and R. Mark, "A Comparative Analysis of Current Credit Risk Models." Paper presented at the Bank of England Conference on Credit Risk Modeling and Regulatory Implications, London, September 21–22, 1998.

Crouhy, M., S.M. Turnbull, and Lee M. Wakeman, "Measuring Risk-Adjusted Performance." Paper presented at Center for Economic Policy Research (CEPR) Conference, London, September 20, 1998.

Delianedis, G., and R. Geske, "Credit Risk and Risk-Neutral Default Probabilities: Information About Rating Migrations and Defaults." Paper presented at the Bank of England Conference on Credit Risk Modeling and Regulatory Implications, London, September 21–22, 1998.

Dermine, J., "Pitfalls in the Application of RAROC in Loan Management." *The Arbitrageur,* Spring 1998, pp. 21–27.

Diebold, F., and R. Mariano, "Comparing Predictive Accuracy." *Journal of Business and Economic Statistics,* May 1995, pp. 253–264.

Duffee, G., "Estimating the Price of Default Risk." *The Review of Financial Studies,* Spring 1999, pp. 197–226.

Duffie, D., and D. Lando, "Term Structures of Credit Spreads with Incomplete Accounting Information." Working Paper, Graduate School of Business, Stanford University, 1997.

Duffie, D., and M. Huang, "Swap Rates and Credit Quality." *Journal of Finance,* July 1996, pp. 921–950.

Duffie, D., and K. Singleton,"Simulating Correlated Defaults." Paper presented at the Bank of England Conference on Credit Risk Modeling and Regulatory Implications, London, September 21–22, 1998.

Elton, E.J., and M.J. Gruber, *Modern Portfolio Theory and Investment Analysis,* 5th Ed. New York: John Wiley & Sons, Inc., 1998.

Estrella, A., "Formulas or Supervision? Remarks on the Future of Regulatory Capital." Paper presented at a Conference on Financial Services at the Crossroads: Capital Regulation in the 21st Century, Federal Reserve Bank of NY, February 26–27, 1998.

Fadil, M.W., "Problems with Weighted-Average Risk Ratings: A Portfolio Management View." *Commercial Lending Review,* January 1997, pp. 23–27.

Federal Reserve System Task Force Report, "Credit Risk Models at Major U.S. Banking Institutions: Current State of the Art and Implications for Assessments of Capital Adequacy." Washington, DC, 1998.

Fehle, F., "Market Structure and Swap Spreads: International Evidence." Working Paper, University of Texas at Austin, September 13, 1998.

Financial Times, "Fears over Banks Prompt Surge in Credit Derivatives," October 7, 1998, p. 1.

Finnerty, J.D., "Credit Derivatives, Infrastructure Finance and Emerging Market Risk." *The Financier,* February 1996, pp. 64–78.

Flannery, M.J., and S. Sorescu, "Evidence of Bank Market Discipline in Subordinated Debenture Yields: 1983–1991." *Journal of Finance,* September 1996, pp. 1347–1377.

Fons, J., "Using Default Rates to Model the Term Structure of Credit Risk." *Financial Analysts Journal,* September–October 1994, pp. 25–32.

General Accounting Office, "Risk-Based Capital: Regulatory and Industry Approaches to Capital and Risk." Washington, DC, General Accounting Office 1998, Report No. 98–153.

Geske, R., "The Valuation of Corporation Liabilities as Compound Options." *Journal of Financial and Quantitative Analysis,* November 1977, pp. 541–552.

Ginzberg, A., K. Maloney, and R. Wilner, "Risk Rating Migration and Valuation of Floating Rate Debt." Working Paper, Citicorp, March 1994.

Gordy, M.B., "A Comparative Anatomy of Credit Risk Models." Paper presented at the Bank of England Conference on Credit Risk Modeling and Regulatory Implications, London, September 21–22, 1998.

Gorton, G., and A. Santomero, "Market Discipline and Bank Subordinated Debt." *Journal of Money, Credit and Banking,* February 1990, pp. 117–128.

Granger, C.W.J., and L.L. Huang, "Evaluation of Panel Data Models: Some Suggestions from Time-Series." Discussion Paper 97-10, Dept. of Economics, University of California, San Diego, 1997.

Harrison, J.M., and S.R. Pliska, "Martingales and Stochastic Integrals." *Stochastic Processes and Their Applications,* August 1981, pp. 215–260.

Harrison, M., *Brownian Motion and Stochastic Flow Systems.* New York: John Wiley & Sons, Inc., 1985.

Harrison, M., and D. Kreps, "Martingales and Arbitrage in Multi-Period Security Markets." *Journal of Economic Theory,* 1979, pp. 381–408.

Hendricks, D., "Netting Agreements and the Credit Exposures of OTC Derivatives Portfolios." *Federal Reserve Bank of New York, Quarterly Review,* Spring 1994, pp. 36–69.

International Swaps and Derivatives Association (ISDA), *Credit Risk and Regulatory Capital,* New York/London, March 1998.

James, C., "RAROC-Based Capital Budgeting and Performance Evaluation: A Case Study of Bank Capital Allocation." University of Florida, 1996 (mimeo).

Jarrow, R., D. Lando, and S. Turnbull, "A Markov Model for the Term Structure of Credit Spreads." *Review of Financial Studies,* 1997, pp. 481–523.

Jarrow, R.A., and S.M. Turnbull, "The Intersection of Market and Credit Risk." Paper presented at the Bank of England Conference on Credit Risk Modeling and Regulatory Implications, September 21–22, London, 1998.

Jarrow, R.A., and D.R. van Deventer, "Practical Usage of Credit Risk Models in Loan Portfolio and Counterparty Exposure Management." The Kamakura Corporation, March 15, 1999 (mimeo).

Jones, D., "Emerging Problems with the Accord: Regulatory Capital Arbitrage and Related Issues." Federal Reserve Board of Governors, July 1998 (mimeo).

Jones, E.P., S.P. Mason, and E. Rosenfeld, "Contingent Claims Analysis of Corporate Capital Structures: An Empirical Investigation." *Journal of Finance*, July 1984, pp. 611–625.

Kealhofer, S., "Managing Default Risk in Derivative Portfolios," in *Derivative Credit Risk: Advances in Measurement and Management*. London: Renaissance Risk Publications, 1995.

KMV, "Credit Monitor Overview." San Francisco: KMV Corporation, 1993 (mimeo).

KMV, "Global Correlation Factor Structure." San Francisco: KMV Corporation, August 1996 (mimeo).

KMV, "KMV and CreditMetrics." San Francisco: KMV Corporation, 1997 (mimeo).

KMV, "Portfolio Management of Default Risk." San Francisco: KMV Corporation, November 15, 1993 (mimeo).

KMV, "Portfolio Manager Model." San Francisco: KMV Corporation, undated.

Koyluoglu, H.U., and A. Hickman, "A Generalized Framework for Credit Risk Portfolio Models." Oliver, Wyman and Co., New York, September 14, 1998.

KPMG, "Loan Analysis System." New York: KPMG Financial Consulting Services, 1998.

KPMG Peat Marwick, *VAR: Understanding and Applying Value-At-Risk*. New York: Risk Publications, 1997.

Kreps, D., "Multiperiod Securities and the Efficient Allocation of Risk: A Comment on the Black–Scholes Option Pricing Model," in J.J. McCall (Ed.), *The Economics of Uncertainty and Information*. Chicago: University of Chicago Press, 1982.

Kuritzkes, A., "Transforming Portfolio Management." *Banking Strategies*, July/August 1998.

Leland, H., "Agency Costs, Risk Management and Capital Structure." *Journal of Finance*, July 1998, pp. 1213–1242.

Leland, H., "Corporate Debt Value, Bond Covenants and Optimal Capital Structure." *Journal of Finance*, September 1994, pp. 1213–1252.

Leland, H., and K. Toft, "Optimal Capital Structure, Endogenous Bankruptcy, and the Term Structure of Credit Spreads." *Journal of Finance*, July 1996, pp. 987–1019.

Litterman, R., and T. Iben, "Corporate Bond Valuation and the Term Structure of Credit Spreads." *Journal of Portfolio Management*, November 3, 1989, pp. 52–64.

Longstaff, F.A., and E.F. Schwartz, "A Simple Approach to Valuing Risky Fixed and Floating Rate Debt." *Journal of Finance*, July 1995, pp. 789–819.

Lopez, J.A., and M.R. Saidenberg, "Evaluating Credit Risk Models." Paper presented at the Bank of England Conference on Credit Risk Modeling and Regulatory Implications, September 21–22, 1998.

Madan, D.B., and H. Unal, "Pricing the Risks of Default." University of Maryland, College Park, Dept. of Finance, 1994 (mimeo).

McAllister, P.M., and J.J. Mingo, "Commercial Loan Risk Management, Credit Scoring and Pricing: The Need for a New Shared Database." *Journal of Commercial Lending*, May 1994, pp. 6–20.

McKinsey and Co., *Credit Portfolio View*. New York: McKinsey and Co., 1997.

McQuown, J.A., "The Illuminated Guide to Portfolio Management." *Journal of Lending and Credit Risk Management*, August 1997, pp. 29–41.

McQuown, J.A., "Market vs. Accounting-Based Measures of Default Risk." San Francisco: KMV Corporation, 1995.

McQuown, J.A., and S. Kealhofer, "A Comment on the Formation of Bank Stock Prices." San Francisco: KMV Corporation, April 1997.

Mella-Barral, P., and W. Perraudin, "Strategic Debt Service." *Journal of Finance*, June 1997, pp. 531–556.

Merrill Lynch, "Credit Default Swaps." New York: Global Fixed Income Research, October 1998.

Merton, R.C., "On the Pricing of Corporate Debt: The Risk Structure of Interest Rates." *Journal of Finance*, June 1974, pp. 449–470.

Miller, R., "Refining Ratings." *Risk Magazine*, August 1998.

Mingo, J.J., "Policy Implications of the Federal Reserve Study of Credit Risk Models at Major Banking Institutions." Paper presented at the Bank of England Conference on Credit Risk Modeling and Regulatory Implications, London, September 21–22, 1998.

Morgan, J.P., *CreditMetrics*. New York: Technical Document, April 2, 1997.

Nickell, P., W. Perraudin, and S. Varotto, "Stability of Rating Transitions." Paper presented at the Bank of England Conference on Credit Risk Modeling and Regulatory Implications, London, September 21–22, 1998.

Oda, N., and J. Muranaga, "A New Framework for Measuring the Credit Risk of a Portfolio: The 'ExVAR' Model." Monetary and Economic Studies, Bank of Japan, Tokyo, December 1997.

Rajan, R., "Insiders and Outsiders: The Choice between Informed and Arm's Length Debt." *Journal of Finance,* September 1992, pp. 1367–1400.

Ronn, E., and A. Verma, "Pricing Risk-Adjusted Deposit Insurance: An Option-Based Model." *Journal of Finance,* September 1986, pp. 871–896.

Sanvicente, A.S., and F.L.C. Bader, "Filing for Financial Reorganization in Brazil: Event Prediction with Accounting and Financial Variables and the Information Content of the Filing Announcement." Working paper, Sao Paulo University, Sao Paulo, Brazil, March 1996.

Saunders, A., *Financial Institutions Management: A Modern Perspective,* 2nd Ed. BurrRidge, IL: Irwin/McGraw-Hill, 1997.

Saunders, A., A. Srinivasan, and I. Walter, "Price Formation in the OTC Corporate Bond Markets: A Field Study of the Inter-Dealer Market." Working Paper No. 98-89, Dept. of Finance, NYU, 1998.

Shearer, A., "Pricing for Risk Is the Key in Commercial Lending." *American Banker,* March 21, 1997, p. 1.

Shepheard-Walwyn, T., and R. Litterman, "Building a Coherent Risk Measurement and Capital Optimization Model for Financial Firms." Paper presented at the Conference on Financial Services at the Crossroads: Capital Regulation in the 21st Century, New York, February 26–27, 1998.

Shimko, D., N. Tejima, and D.R. van Deventer, "The Pricing of Risky Debt when Interest Rates Are Stochastic." *Journal of Fixed Income,* September 1993, pp. 58–66.

Smith, C.W., W. Smithson, and D.S. Wilford, *Managing Financial Risk.* Cambridge, MA: Ballinger, 1990.

Society of Actuaries, "1986–1992 Credit Loss Experience Study: Private Placement Bonds." Schaumburg, IL: 1996.

Stahl, G., "Confidence Intervals for Different Capital Definitions in a Credit Risk Model." Paper presented at Center for Economic Policy Research (CEPR) Conference, London, September 20, 1998.

Standard and Poor's, "Rating Performance 1997—Stability and Transition." New York: Standard and Poor's Research Report, 1998.

Stiglitz, J., and A. Weiss, "Credit Rationing in Markets with Imperfect Information." *American Economic Review,* June 1981, pp. 393–410.

Sundaram, R.K., "Equivalent Martingale Measures and Risk-Neutral Pricing: An Expository Note." *Journal of Derivatives,* Fall 1997, pp. 85–98.

Taylor, J.D., "Cross-Industry Differences in Business Failure Rates: Implications for Portfolio Management." *Commercial Lending Review,* January 1998, pp. 36–46.

Treacy, W., and M. Carey, "Internal Credit Risk Rating Systems at Large U.S. Banks." *Federal Reserve Bulletin,* November 1998.

Vasicek, O., "Probability of Loss on a Loan Portfolio." San Francisco: KMV Corporation, undated (mimeo).

Wall, L., and M.M. Shrikhande, "Credit Derivatives." Paper presented at the FMA Conference, Chicago, October 1998.

Wilson, T., "Credit Risk Modeling: A New Approach." New York: McKinsey Inc., 1997a (mimeo).

Wilson, T., "Portfolio Credit Risk (Parts I and II)." *Risk Magazine,* September and October, 1997b.

Zaik, E., J. Walter, and J.G. Kelling, "RAROC at Bank of America: From Theory to Practice." *Journal of Applied Corporate Finance,* Summer 1996, pp. 83–93.

Zhou, C., "A Jump Diffusion Approach to Modeling Credit Risk and Valuing Defaultable Securities." Working Paper, Federal Reserve Board of Governors, undated 1997.

Index